Watchfires

RESCUE PRESS

CHICAGO, CLEVELAND, IOWA CITY

Copyright © 2016 Hilary Plum

Printed in the United States of America

First Edition

ISBN 978-0-9860869-5-3

Design by Sevy Perez

Cover by Alex Kostiw and Sevy Perez

Chaparral Pro

rescuepress.co

Watchfires

Hilary Plum

TO MY PARENTS

I

"There are places no history can reach"

"War feels to me an oblique place"

DID HE SPEAK *with an accent?* She looked up. Between her and the screen were arrangements of chairs which bodies occupied nervously. No, the interviewee said, he sounded just like you and me. Things we'd talk about would be like which rapper was best.

Onscreen people used the phrase *tight-knit community*. Here in the waiting room unironically a woman knitted.

*

In the theater he was unconscious. Is there an *I* to the anesthetized body? To the still-beating heart or the mechanism, halted, of peri-

11

stalsis? My belly was opened three times; through the largest incision they removed the large intestine. He would say: I had colon cancer. He is thirty years old.

Four months ago his father had died of cancer born in the colon. His father's father had died of cancer at forty-one, his father in turn at thirty-three. How fortunate we are to live in an age of advanced detection. In the waiting room she opened her book, which could be called a masterpiece of the Palestinian catastrophe: the plight of the refugees, the failures of the resistance.

*

Four days ago and four hundred miles away two bombs had detonated. How may we describe it? Her brother had lived for years in that city and still she could only drive anywhere there if she started at that yuppie hardware store. Like hundreds of thousands she'd been a student on the city's outskirts. Once a year it was Marathon Monday and for days after the cheering no one on campus could speak. She'd once jumped into the race to help pace a friend and had ducked out just before the finish line. At the finish line two bombs exploded. Thirteen years passed between these moments, though as the race measured time they were close: the difference between nine and nine and a half minutes per mile. There were two bombs, first one, then the other. There were two brothers, one older, one younger.

There were cameras everywhere and later the brothers would appear on every channel: baseball caps and zip-up jackets, dark nylon backpacks, boy and man walking around a corner, or standing facing the race amid the crowd.

By the time she learned the brothers' names the older was dead, a *shootout with the police*. The boy was, what is the phrase, *in the wind*? A manhunt. A lockdown. Do not leave your homes, the governor instructed the people of the city. Onscreen every few minutes a police spokesman approached a microphone. The trains had stopped running, the buses, cars. In certain neighborhoods SWAT teams were checking each room of each residence.

Upon hearing the name of one neighborhood she stepped outside to call a friend. Her friend said: The SWAT team came through at 6 AM. We ran out of wine at 9.

*

The novel she read was in English, though it had been written in no language she knew. Such transformations are possible. The cancer was caused by a genetic mutation; no, the mutation was linked to a high incidence of cancer, a statistical likelihood. If someone knew precisely how this mutation caused tumors, or allowed tumors, or fostered—it wasn't she; she didn't have even a verb. His father had had the mutation and so, one might assume, did his father, and his. To think that when in that last winter they had helped the father into and out of bed, his legs swollen beyond what she could have imagined, his hiccups, which jolted exactly the site of the tumor, a continual torment, to think that even then in the belly of the son the offspring of the father's tumor was growing, feeding on the nourishment meant for every good cell, every other cell.

Could it be called a blessing, that the father had died without knowing of this inheritance? He had endured so much, surely he could have borne this news, he would have recognized the gift he had helped offer: he had lived long enough, through three occurrences of cancer, for science to discover this mutation, a knowledge in which his body was incorporated and which might save, might right now be saving, the life of his son. After death what trace remains of one's knowledge, the lifetime of knowledge one is said—in English—to have possessed?

Is it a coincidence, the word *cell*? A terrorist cell? the newscasters wondered all morning, the long hours authorities hunted the boy. A sleeper cell? Did they act alone?

*

That day in the waiting room she had occasion to consider coincidences. Her first novel had just been published, a novel she had written a few years before, during the height of the Iraq War. In the novel a group of Americans undertake (this the verb she'd used in the obligatory descriptions) a series of bombings to protest the war. The brother of one activist served in Iraq and upon returning home commits suicide. One of the activists will die as a result of one of his own bombs.

Since the marathon bombing friends had been writing her. Was there something prescient to the novel? So far the only radical ideas the brothers, authors of the bombing, had been known to espouse was an opposition to the US wars in Iraq and Afghanistan. That and the facts, widely noted, that they were Muslim and immigrants: their father was Chechen and after a life as refugees in Kyrgyzstan and Russia they had come to the US in 2002. Chechnya, a land known for its sufferings, its terrorism or resistance, let's use both words for now, the news ceaseless and the operation taking hours, long enough to imagine every disaster. She imagines his death; together the screen and the book in her lap testify to almost every possible horror, but in this moment she fears only his death. Now someone has located the father of the bombers, who had returned to Russia a few years ago, he was sick and wished to be sick among family in a city of refugees and not in America. The father believed nothing said of his boys, and such love might hearten were it not terrifying, that a father could out of love deny any and all evidence, evidence his sons offered in word and deed.

Not prescience, but coincidence—not chance, but simultaneity. She was American *born and bred*, but she too had felt a current of rage move through her. She had remained within the borders of the novel, an imagined territory. She had not bought a pressure cooker, packed it with ball bearings, set the backpack down among cheering families, restaurant managers, for instance, international students, eight-year-olds. Copley Square, the Boston Public Library, the anniversary of the shot heard round the world. The novel she had written had nothing to do with the boy whose face appeared always so young on the screen. But could emotion be a current into which strangers swim, their limbs brush one another's, their limbs tangle? There are words for emotions felt in common: patriotism; or the anxiety of this waiting room; or the standby *Zeitgeist*. In the waiting room she spoke to no one, other than one elderly man volunteer, who twice offered her tea just as she was lifting a mug of coffee to her lips.

In a moment of reflection a pundit observed that the brothers' opposition to the war in Iraq was evidence of nothing, since a majority of Americans held this same view.

*

The logic of two consecutive bombs: the second targets those who have rushed to help the victims of the first. So common is this strategy that it shadows the very words *first responder*.

*

In the first days after the bombing she had joined the many who called the brothers cowards. Not the brothers, not yet—but the idea of the guilty men. One may assume they were men. She had thought—as though she ought to have an opinion—that the bombers might belong to a racist militant group, since these were said to be growing in number in the years since Obama's election. And Boston was well known for the racism of its past, its present. Could a place be seen as racist—its brick-row buildings, package stores, ludicrous one-ways, dirty river and students sculling, bars, the green monster, the accents? The brothers were white, though at one point they were called dark-skinned; at one point a Saudi man fleeing the explosion, covered in others' blood, was stopped by police.

This—the fate of the Saudi man—was what she meant: shouldn't the guilty have picked up the phone? Was there no code of honor? Didn't the IRA, didn't Hamas, Islamic Jihad, who knows who? Al-Qaeda had at least through its actions made its rhetoric clear: no question as to what they were targeting, the heart they meant to pierce. But this, these hobbyist runners whose legs were now amputated, the dead a child and two young women, what was this to mean? If the terrorists didn't say, was this not a waste? An immoral economy but there it was: they had three dead and over two hundred injured, currency to buy their cause airtime. They had only to pick up the phone. But either they were too frightened or didn't know what to say of what they'd done. A coward's silence, two cowards' silence.

The brothers, it seems, had not thought they'd be traced and had made no plans to elude capture. This naivety did not endear them.

A conclusion: it would be better to kill oneself. In this thought she was not alone. If this rage inspired such violence, required such violence, shouldn't one offer oneself as fuel?

Most people don't know that suicide bombing became a central strategy of the Palestinian resistance only after the Cave of the Patriarchs massacre in 1994, when a Jewish American doctor from Brooklyn entered the Mosque of Abraham during morning prayer and with a machine gun killed twenty-nine Palestinians, wounded one hundred and twenty-five. But what do most people know?

Recently a massage therapist had asked her, embarrassed, whether Germany was our ally.

Every cause aims to harness the passion of youth. Conscripts; suicide bombers. At least in an army many survived. Even in the attacks of September 11 it was the young men who sacrificed themselves; their elders survived, to be later tortured or killed, it's true, and not in a time or place of their choosing, no choice what prayer or lack of would be on their lips when they were struck down. Of the two brothers the younger, nineteen, lived. By the time she read of his capture her husband had awoken, attached to a million machines. The boy had left a bloody trail to a boat in someone's backyard, the homeowner had peeked under the tarp to discover him. The boy had been shot in the mouth and could not speak; in response to his interrogation he passed notes. Did he write with an accent?

HOW MANY VETERANS commit suicide each day? American veterans, that is.

*

How to think of Americans as refugees without destroying the word. In Boston how many thousands called themselves Irish. In this waiting room she could be called an outsider. Everyone else, or nearly, was from this rural stretch of central Pennsylvania, and she had lived here only a year and a half and that reluctantly. As soon as her husband recovered they would leave; a new job awaited him in Philadelphia. He worked in academia, and they had moved among college towns, like her parents, like herself these thirty-two years: New York, Vermont, Connecticut, Massachusetts, New York, Massachusetts, Pennsylvania. His father had worked in local and state government, which at a certain level required a specialist not in the place but the work: Virginia, Michigan, Washington, Maryland. She read of the lost Palestinian villages, and though she remembered well the green of her childhood and the smell of manure she loved and which this town had returned to her, she had no experience of home and home-lessness in common with those villagers, now refugees, now children of refugees, born and raised in the camps. Her home was something like this: in this waiting room, she read a novel. If all of those waiting had had to arise and, pins handed round, place Chechnya on a map, she could have won the game. She belonged to a sort of academic class, an intelligentsia, though who uses this word now. She felt at home in any college library. This confession may not be endearing. She was mobile. More than one-third of Americans live their whole lives within the same town, another fifth within the same state.

A friend from South Africa used to ask her to pronounce the North-east's Native American names. *Ticonderoga*, she said for him, *Winni-pesaukee*. Like many white South Africans of his generation he had emigrated and did not hope to return, betrayed by his country, the apartheid regime was overthrown only when he was a teenager, who could forgive a nation for implicating one from birth onward in such atrocity. He had never said this to her; if asked he might say something different. Over the years she had stopped noticing how different the names of places were from any other word she pronounced. This difference appealed to him, and to her, once she considered it—she had wondered at it as a child—although or because they both recognized this difference as evidence of absence, of genocide. She used to read a poet well known in the sixties and seventies who claimed that until America faced its ghosts, the specters of the indigenous people it had massacred and subjected, it would keep waging war against brown-skinned people worldwide. This sort of psychological/mythical theory was of its time and yet still gave one pause.

*

When she had stood before a wall of soldiers' faces in the museum at Gettysburg, so many hundreds of photographs, she had felt certain of her allegiance. The Union *us*, the Confederates *them*. There was no pattern by which one could distinguish the faces of one from those of the other, and had a mischievous curator switched the labels dividing the wall she would not have known.

Conclusion, obvious: war can be relied upon as a means for youth to destroy youth, as a productive means to dispose of the poor. In felling the rich, the middle class, the bankers and lawyers and government workers, the wives and daughters, terrorism violates the code.

Since almost all violence is perpetrated by men, the history of violence is sometimes, more radically, called a history of men at war against women. This thought was not original to her but it was unsettling, as the weather warmed and the catcalls of spring commenced.

*

Four years ago the older brother had been arrested for domestic assault and battery. He hit her lightly, the father said. It may have been for this reason that his application for US citizenship was delayed; that or the suspicions of the FBI and the Russian FSB.

*

In college, in a course on love, she had been taught that even the great pacifists believed in self-defense. Nonviolence was right for social movements, for any cause, any nation or would-be nation, but if they come to your lawn, your home, your body: defend yourself. She agreed. The problem arose in how one defined the self.

*

She wanted to present herself to the surgeons and say: He is mine. Any error you make, the loss will be mine. Surely they understood this; this was their work. She liked that their scrubs were undignified, allied them not with the workaday world but with their patients: gowned, bare-assed and slack-jawed, every kind of fluid pumped in and out or leaking. Surgeons never wear gloves, his mother observed days later, meaning not for surgery but the exams: a surgeon had been by his room and examined the incision barehanded.

They might think of the incision as theirs, since they had made it, since their hands had spent hours in this torso, and this line of staples, bruised and crusting darkly, was the trace left of their action. Now their fingers prospecting freely a wound in this room, the next, the next. To protect ourselves against ourselves; to protect what is ours from ourselves, and vice versa.

*

For twelve years she'd had a *chronic illness* and for the last five she had not been *financially independent*. If not for her husband's good middle-class job she'd have applied for federal disability. Disabled as citizen: member of a nation, unable. *Martyr* would be a more dignified label, but not appropriate; no intention could offer her suffering to a cause.

Twelve years had passed since the April she had first collapsed. She was running and went down mid-stride. Looking like, a friend said, one of those cheap toys: press the base of the platform and the creature on top slumps over. The illness was neurological and these past three years had been worsening. It came on in what she called *episodes*, between which she was fine. Lately there had been little time between; lately it had been a sort of siege, but in place of the drama that word might suggest, an ungovernable dullness. When sick she couldn't read or write or work and could barely walk, passed her days on the couch or in bed watching television or skimming a mystery novel or a book meant for children. Days, weeks, months thus confined. Since she saw few people when she was ill, most people knew only, she came to believe, one version of her: the one who was out in the world and seemed, we might say, *normal*. She could speak of the other life she lived, confined all those days, but it felt like a story, something people would nod to but then ask the wrong question, and since her illness had yet to be definitively diagnosed she didn't have even a name to offer. It had come to feel as though her normal self was a lie, a fiction others welcomed and in which she too believed for hours at a time but which would inevitably dissolve. To others, she thought, it seemed as if she were one of them, when in fact, a jet-setting Persephone, she belonged day by day to a distant kingdom.

And so like everyone she lived two lives, public and private. But for her the division between was exceptionally violent. A claim that may also describe, for instance, the life of a refugee, displaced and living in a foreign country. Not that she and the refugee had an experience in common; but perhaps in the fact of this inexpressible schism— the public cleaved from the private—they might more easily imagine one another.

*

The spring the cancer took root in his gut she got better.

*

A mile and a half from their home was the US Army War College. Military officers attended for advanced degrees; foreign scholars and experts on warfare came to learn and to teach. In yoga class she eavesdropped on the wives of officers. The barracks had its own golf course, around it a gravel path on which she liked to run. The path was marked with adjectives, *friendly*, *courteous*, *responsible*, written on benches or posts that measured the miles. Next to the golf course was an open-air exhibit: here you could walk a three-quarter-mile route and see World War II–era mess tents, Civil War–era battle-field huts, tanks of myriad sizes and decades, howitzers, helicopters with mouths painted on them, teeth bared, a simulacrum of World War I trenches, of World War II concrete bunkers, a simulacrum of a Revolutionary War fort and of a Vietnam War elevated outpost, sandbags and barbed wire, at the end of it all a museum she had never entered. She had imagined the concrete bunkers scarring the face of Europe; in her mind she had filled the trenches with men and mud, insufficiently. She had used the water fountains, the Porta Potties, across from the tanks. Across the street from the golf course's entrance a cemetery was crowded gracelessly by the road, beyond it the barracks and its athletic fields. In the graves were buried children who had not survived their time at the Carlisle Indian Industrial School, which from 1879 to 1918 this town had been famed for. Over 12,000 Native children had been sent to it, from over 140 tribes. Across the country nearly 150 such schools had existed, this their model. *To civilize the Indian, get him into civilization. To keep him civilized, let him stay.* The graves bore the children's English names—Marys and Johns abounded—and the names of their tribes. Had their families sought the graves out, they would have found their children buried under new names in a foreign language, hundreds of miles from home and among endless strangers; that is, how would they have found them. In a novel it would seem too obvious to place the War College and the barracks precisely on the site of the old school and its graveyard, as they were in life.

*

Some say the plague of PTSD has worsened because of technology. In the past the journey home from the battlefront took weeks or months, by foot, horse, boat, train. Together veterans could spend this time transforming themselves from warriors back into husbands and fathers, members of civilian society. Now the journey is a few hours: step off the plane and you must act as though war has ceased, no longer exists. As though who you were there and all you suffered was safe in the past.

*

Soon cries will commence to try the boy, a citizen, one of us, as an *enemy combatant*. Most who now bear that label are imprisoned, without trial, off-shore in that prison not legal enough for American soil. This spring one hundred prisoners are on hunger strike; to feed them twice a day navy medics force a tube down the noses and into the stomachs of the recalcitrant.

Soon she will be buying cough drops for her husband, his throat raw from just such a tube, his nose bleeding.

Every competent patient, the code of doctors states, *has the right to refuse medical intervention, including life-sustaining interventions.*

WHAT HAPPENED TO the boy? What changed him? These were the questions the news pored over, in ceaseless stylized pronouncements from talking heads, whose highlights and shoulder pads and soft-bellied suits streamed all day over the television's surface. The metaphor was of a poison lurking among us, within us, in the body of our nation. Living like our neighbor, accepting our welfare checks, attending our schools, speaking our language, and then, without warning, attacking. A cancer. You might say.

On the news they agreed on a story: the younger brother had looked up to the older; the man had influenced the boy. The boy had *assimilated* and the man had not. But what if the boy's adoration was the

vital element? Without the love of the boy, the man was a failed boxer, a wife beater, a thug. When he saw himself in his brother's eyes
his rage possessed new grandeur and new possibility. He formulated
the plan not just for its own sake but for the fact of his brother walking into the crowd three steps behind him, each sliding a backpack
off his shoulders. There is no proof of this, but it is a story. And now
only one brother remains. What can he tell us? If he had the choice,
he might have preferred silence, preferred death. He must know
that he did have that choice.

*

Twenty-two each day. Every sixty-five minutes an American veteran
takes his or her life.

*

As a teenager she'd suffered from anorexia nervosa, a compulsion toward self-starvation widespread among young women of her background and class. (The disease is presently increasing among men
and across the urbanizing world.) One-fifth to one-third of sufferers
will eventually die of the disease, the highest mortality rate of any

mental disorder. The media and its obsession with appearance, its idolization of extreme thinness, are most often blamed. A war on women's bodies; the lies, unceasing and everywhere, perpetrated by Photoshop (when she was a girl it was *airbrushing*).

The two illnesses she has suffered are existentially distinct. One was an emotional disorder, or psychological; one is neurological. Those who treat them have little to do with each other. The first is a disease of the mind, or, speaking poetically, the heart; the second of the brain. In the case of the first you may be held responsible, as both agent and victim of your own destruction. In the case of the second you are simply victim: passive, struck down.

For the first few years her anorexia had been misdiagnosed. She'd told family and doctors that she had an *upset stomach* and this was why she'd lost weight, why she kept getting thinner. This was partly true, but mostly not; she was surprised when for years no one called her bluff. Her doctor, a gastroenterologist, had seemed accomplished: recently he'd been in the paper for his work in the cancer ward, photographed surrounded by tiny bald children holding popsicles. After a colonoscopy he concluded she had Crohn's disease, a chronic inflammatory condition in which the immune system mounts continual attacks on the normal, beneficial bacteria in the gut. The summer she was fourteen she was hospitalized; she stood five feet five inches and weighed eighty-six pounds.

Throughout the ninth grade she spent twelve hours a day on a feeding tube. At 6 PM she threaded the tube up her nose and down her throat, and—until in time she became expert—checked its position in her stomach with a stethoscope. She dragged a pole hung with sacks of Ensure behind her through the house and when the machine beeped in the night she woke to pour in more cans of beige nutrition. At 6 AM she untaped the tube from her cheek and yanked it out of her nose, tasting each morning her stomach acid. She went to school. Only a handful of friends knew her secret; or perhaps everyone knew.

At the rate the tube pumped calories into her she would reach her target weight in seven weeks, her doctor had said, and showed her the math on his notepad. It was not of course *her* target weight, but his. She only wanted the numbers on the scale to decrease and herself to diminish. He was proved wrong: it took at least nine months for her to gain enough, and this was a triumph of her resistance. She followed the regimen she was prescribed but did what she could to sabotage it. In this way her agency manifested itself through stead-fast self-destruction. She has sometimes considered this irony a tes-tament to the spirit of the nineties, she a child of her time; but such irony flourishes across epochs.

The doctor had forbidden her from joining the high-school swim team as she wished, declaring this too much exercise for their calor-ic equations. Yet, absurdly, he allowed her to run. Just four or five miles a day, he said—which as soon as he pronounced it became her goal; she had never run anything like this distance. The town where she lived was rural and beautiful but every day she ran only around the track, sixteen to twenty laps in the sun. She had never enjoyed running and now lap after lap abhorred it.

When she looks back on this time, the doctor's frustration as each visit she failed to measure up, to meet her mark on the scale, her silence as she sat in his office, feet dangling off the examination bed, she feels that they were both complicit. That although he stuck to his story—Crohn's disease, to be treated with steroids and enteral feeding—he knew that this was no more than a battle of wills. He did not want to admit defeat to a ninety-pound girl and so would not acknowledge her victories: that she wouldn't gain weight if she did not wish to; and that as soon—and this is what occurred—as she did, as soon as she returned the feeding tube to his office in celebration, she would lose all the weight again with extraordinary rapidity. Yet this is only a feeling. She has no way to know what he thought that drawn-out year; if he has thought of her since, she can't say of what she has become an example.

She does know that she has never had Crohn's disease. Later doctors looked at the same biopsies and shook their heads: clearly negative. They could not explain why their colleague had been so mistaken and, following a gentleman's code, did not quite criticize him.

At thirty, desperate at her poor health, she underwent one more colonoscopy—what if, she'd thought, the old fool was right?

He wasn't. She does have him to thank for what came to be her love of running, which sustained her through the rest of high school and into college, to the day she collapsed on the track.

*

Even the Prophet Muhammad considered suicide: after receiving the first revelation, overcome with fear, he thought to throw himself from a mountaintop. From the heavens the angel Gabriel cried out to stop him.

*

Upon her recovery from anorexia, she wished to know: how could so many go mad in precisely the same way? Her illness had felt so intimate: she had decided to diet; she dieted; she didn't stop. She had not endeavored to be *anorexic*; it had been years before she even owned up to that word. She'd chosen no model and acted quite alone; yet she'd fit precisely the common pattern.

She read theorists who argued that anorexia arises as response to conflicts over women's role in society. Young women, on the verge of maturation, perceive the troubled path before them: to be a mother or to work? To do both and to fail? Independent or dependent? Virgin, mother, whore? Object of anyone's desire or no one's? Short hair, long, shaven, unshaven... Seeing this storm of choices on the horizon, the anorexic tries to stop time. She sheds weight and her periods cease; she approaches androgyny. She halts herself on the threshold of fertility, of womanhood; she will not enter. If women's realm is the home and the hearth its center, in refusing food and fertility she will refuse the language of women, of her own mother. Instead silence, unto death.

A coward's silence?

Sometimes she has thought so. Unkindly she has thought this most often upon failing to be of help to other anorexics, older than she when taken ill. There was so little one could do; many efforts went poorly. Shouldn't they just grow up? she found herself thinking: Accept that everyone must eat and stop playing these games? A game no one wins, since victory is nonexistence.

Some claim that, like alcoholics, anorexics should only be called *recovering*, never *recovered*. She can't agree. To recover, most alcoholics stop drinking; they mark the days, months, years they've been clean. For the anorexic there's no such purity. Every day, every few hours, she must choose again what to eat. She must choose to eat.

*

There must be other theories of anorexia's origins and meaning, but her research ceased some fifteen years ago; she considers the disease in the terms and metaphors she learned then. She won't begin again, try to see it anew, tell the story differently.

But this isn't true: sometimes she catches herself thinking of those years as a possession. She was possessed. By some malign spirit of the age she lived in. When she with great effort exorcised it from herself, she felt as if—forgive the metaphor—she was awaking from a nightmare into the light. Was the disease herself or was she diseased? Who was it who so endangered this body, terrorized her family three times a day, drove her mother into desperation, had so little mercy? She was sick. Did a demon possess her? It was she.

*

Of the one hundred seventy-one men still imprisoned that spring in Guantanamo Bay, eighty-nine have been cleared for release. But what should be done with them, where will they go? It seems more than a decade has been required to answer these questions, though many answers would do. They remain imprisoned, no end in sight.

Two months into the hunger strike, forty more military medics were shipped to the camp to help keep its prisoners alive, a task that now requires the use of force.

A few years ago forty prisoners were released to be resettled in six-teen countries. These are called *third countries*: the first being their home; the second, it seems, the United States. The US imprisoned them; but they were never there.

Some prisoners say the present strike was sparked by a shakedown in which guards mishandled prisoners' Qur'ans. Authorities deny this. *They feel like they're living in graves*, one lawyer noted on a recent visit.

They won't let us live in peace, and they won't let us die in peace.

*

The brothers might have learned strategy close to home. In Afghan-istan and Pakistan the US has deployed drones to strike those who'd gathered to aid the victims of the strike before.

*

It's not that each explanation requires metaphor; it's that each ex-planation is only metaphor. Metaphorically speaking, are we now in the age of autoimmune disease? Now the enemy is ourselves: we can no longer tell friend from foe; we mistake self for other. Help-less we mount full-force attacks against ourselves. (If the body could speak—could defend itself—would it name this a *preemptive strike*?)

*

Her husband will spend ten days in the hospital and she will be there every day. She'll read three novels, suck on hard candies, and walk through the field surrounding the hospital complex. Each morning she'll bathe him: he'll stand in the bathroom hunched with pain and attached to an IV pole, and she'll fill a basin with sudsy water and with a washcloth clean the bruised skin of his back and torso, the bruise that extends from his incision in every direction. In his mor-phined bluntness he corrects her technique. Her intimacy with his body seems less than useful; the skill lies not in tending to one's husband but in tending to any vulnerable body.

Right before he's released a surgeon comes by and, displeased with the discharge of a hematoma, plucks out seven or eight of the couple dozen stitches that bind the incision. You'll just have to pack these sites with gauze, he says, pointing to the holes he has created, bright red gashes.

At home the next morning they realize the nature of their task: to stuff a thumb's worth of gauze right into these chasms in the belly. She watches her husband's fingers disappear into his own torso and understands why people faint at such sights. What should be invisible made suddenly visible. Rupture, violation.

*

Some doctors have diagnosed her with autoimmune disease, or rather, they gave her this name tentatively, a gesture to help her account for her body's failings. You may have had a viral infection, they've said, and this *triggered* an autoimmune response. You may have had a bacterial infection, and this *triggered* an autoimmune response.

She never believed them; these stories did not feel true to her. Though her feelings were not meant to matter, these diagnoses not meant as faith claims.

*

One doctor would name her illness *channelopathy*—disorder of the ion channels—and note that research had traced a handful of channelopathies to particular genetic mutations. It was posited that there could be, must be, many more such disorders, some of the mutations contained within single families: a family might possess its own disease. Of her flawed heritage she might be the sole living incarnation.

Consider her husband's case: if they hadn't known of this mutation, it would have been years before they looked for the cancer that was already there.

*

Some diseases may be called diseases of Westernization. Eating disorders. Crohn's disease, much more common in cities than rural areas, in the global North than the global South. Colon cancer primarily afflicts those in the developed world.

In the case of multiple sclerosis—also autoimmune—occurrence increases with distance from the equator. If one is born in a high-risk region and before reaching puberty moves to a low-risk region, one assumes the new, lower risk of occurrence. But if one moves after puberty, one's risk remains high. For this phenomenon there is no firm explanation.

*

The boy was eight when he came to the US. The man was sixteen.

WHAT COULD SHE say of the time she spent confined?

To wake up and know from the head's leaden state that the day is already lost. She reads detective novels by the dozens. She is employed part-time as an editor and when sick she can't work; once illness has dropped its veil between her and world, her and any text, no effort on her part can break through. But she can, at least sometimes, skim; she can half-read. She needs a book with a good plot, in which one needn't attend to each or any sentence. Instead the weakened mind may wash over the page, or is it the page that washes over the mind. She wants a novel that begins with a body, proceeds until the crime's been solved.

She just needs to be well enough every few mornings, before the worst sets in, to walk to the library and check out a new stack. If she has a book, if she can pass the time. If she doesn't have to watch TV eight or ten hours a day. She can survive. What does she mean, *survive*? She couldn't defend the word but it's what she feels.

Detective fiction, a favorite essay puts it, *asserts social optimism, a triumph over grim context. Detective stories are not about guilt and innocence, that is, not about morality; they are about details. The clue is a detail that solves a specific crime when appropriately observed by a detecting person....*

The point of detection is to uncover the incontrovertible relationship between logic and justice. In the course of being detected, things—that is, objects, events, and ideas—that seem arbitrary and indiscriminate are rendered logical and relevant.

The nature of the detail, the foregrounding of certain details and their transformation into clues, forces the trivial to become moral, even humanitarian.

*

The man had been a talented boxer and won several regional titles. One year a rule was changed, and he could no longer advance to the national tournament: he was not a citizen, and only citizens were welcome. He quit boxing.

*

After he came to the US as a child, the boy never left again. But the man had gone to Russia a year before the attacks, stayed six months, a visit now to be well scrutinized. Did he meet with militants, fundamentalists? Was it there that he was *radicalized*? Was it by, as the internet claims, the CIA? His parents say he spent his time there at home, with family, reading novels.

*

Her least favorite story: in your youth a tick bit you and passed into your blood these bacteria. You got sick—a rash, a fever—and those symptoms transformed into the ailment, diffuse and mysterious, that has now lasted years. At this point you would test negative on most tests for tick-borne disease, even though this infection is the source of all your suffering.

It's true that she spent her youth in the woods of New England, quite near where this disease was first discovered. All summer dark splotches dotted the floors of her childhood home: ticks who'd over-fed and fell off the cats and dog to burst. These were not even the ones to fear; the danger was in those that were too small to see.

This disease was a source of controversy. All of medicine knew the initial infection: Lyme disease. But this other chronic state, an infection gone underground, immunological hell—this was not *recognized in the literature*. Many believed wholeheartedly in its existence; they protested the medical authorities who doubted it; to offer evidence they organized and maintained websites. A few women, each extremely ill, had told her that this was their diagnosis and probably hers. You can't go to just any doctor, they said. Many won't even treat you. They spoke of the years they'd spent on antibiotics and tinctures, the specialists in this condition they'd been fortunate to find.

She skimmed their blogs. She skimmed because this was all she could do (who reads the endless blogs of the sick? The sick can barely read, barely write, barely think) and because she wished to avoid contact with their words. She was curious but wanted to keep everything about or of them—their terrible suffering, the name they gave it and with which they would name her, *chronic Lyme*— far from her. She wondered at herself; she could not defend how in her mind she estranged herself from them. Was this an act of self-defense? What limits to empathy might survival require? She closed her eyes, clicked shut the window onscreen, refused to be named one of them, she was not one of them, she was of the world, she was us.

It was not that one doubted the fact of their suffering, only the explanation. And yet. Was this not still condescension, condemnation? Some doctors said that this disease was a false category; all the men and women who claimed to have it had other illnesses they'd collectively misunderstood. Some doctors dismissed them, it's true, as not really sick, or at least not physically. In medical terms, a *conversion disorder*: psychological problems transformed into physical suffering, without even the sufferer's knowledge or intent.

I never had a fever, never had a rash, she wrote. *I always tested negative.* She was told that this didn't matter. In this way this diagnosis was a faith claim; once you decide it's true there's only proof, everywhere. You pick your side. She refused. These women are so much sicker than I, she said, I am not one of them, she persuaded herself, even as she grew sicker and no other explanation appeared.

It was almost easier to sympathize with the boy: his thin face, unruly hair, outthrust chin. One could imagine his flaw—to have made the wrong choice. I could make the wrong choice. Subject of the wrong predicate, I. A brother's persuasion, a heartless day.

What no one wished to imagine was no choice. To be made no one, to be confined, within walls, within barbed wire, within an inert body, to live within the grave. We mourn the bombing's victims but we do not know them as ourselves. We think: what if she had been my daughter, my neighbor? Not: what if she had been I, she is I. She ought to feel the most for these sick women but she cannot bear to. They do not seem to recover; when sometimes she thinks of them she finds that their blogs have been silent for months, for years.

To become moral, even humanitarian. She knows that with this phrase the writer means the arc of the detective novel's plot; but she thinks of it otherwise. At the word *humanitarian* she thinks of what detective fiction has offered her all those dreary days, dreary years: relief from suffering.

*

For six days every cemetery refused to inter the man's body. A funeral home had prepared it and was now faced with protestors. The man's wife did not step forward. City after city refused. Finally a place was found, a Muslim cemetery in Virginia. *Jesus tells us, love your enemies*, a statement explained to the press.

*

You might know *conversion disorder* by its former name, *hysteria*.

One doctor has given her this diagnosis. The others disagreed but some still include it occasionally in their notes, usually at the bottom of a list, perhaps with a question mark. Since there is no way to test for such an ailment she does not know when or how the question may be answered.

*

Although she could say that doctors have failed her, she is not a skeptic. Of *chronic Lyme* she cannot believe, as some do, that evidence of the disease has been deliberately suppressed. She believes in error, ineptitude, futility. Of conspiracy theories there is always the hard fact that anyone who believes in one is likely to believe in more, including those that contradict each other. So that each belief becomes testament not only to its subject but to a wider and itself questionable skepticism. A *healthy skepticism*, an *unhealthy*?

Idk why it's hard for many of you to accept that 9/11 was an inside job, I mean I guess fuck the facts y'all are some real #patriots #gethip

This was discovered among the boy's tweets. You could say she helped midwife this theory. She has worked nine years (hours decreasing with her poor health) as an editor with a press that has published some twelve books on what's called *9/11 truth*: the claim that 9/11 was an inside job, a *false-flag operation* perpetrated by the Bush administration as pretense for wars it hoped to launch in the Middle East, its push for regime change and control of oil reserves, the launch of a *New American Century*. This last—the Project for the New American Century—the name of a neoconservative think tank that held great sway in George W. Bush's government. Indeed, within one of the project's policy papers, written well before 9/11, this line appears: *Further, the process of transformation, even if it brings revolutionary change, is likely to be a long one, absent some catastrophic and catalyzing event—like a new Pearl Harbor.*

Like a new Pearl Harbor—evidence to some of guilt, to others merely (merely?) of a profound cynicism and opportunism. It would be hard to argue that the transformative opportunities afforded by 9/11 were not thoroughly exploited: war in Afghanistan, war in Iraq, the PATRIOT Act, the prison at Guantanamo Bay, extraordinary renditions, black-site prisons, torture, warrantless wiretapping, drone warfare, the rise of a vast new national-security apparatus, the collapse of all work to prevent climate change...

The press where she works was founded in the late '80s by an immigrant to the US, a Palestinian born (his family refugees) in Lebanon. He'd wanted to publish Arabic novels in English and for some twenty-five years now he had. The press had a number of trade lists as well—nonfiction, cookbooks, children's books, travel—and for years the travel list had paid most of the bills, that is, until 9/11, the decrease in travel that occurred in its wake. Shortly thereafter they had published their first work of 9/11 truth and were surprised at its success. More volumes followed.

She did not know even now if or to what extent her colleagues believed the books' arguments. They agreed the books could be *quite compelling*; they might feel that publishing them contributed to the health of the democracy. But did they believe the Twin Towers had been brought down not by the planes but in a perfectly timed controlled explosion, the president's finger, as it were, on the red button? That what hit the Pentagon was no plane but a missile?

What would these books' diligent authors think if they knew that even their own publishers might tolerate them, but not believe them? Just what does the boy believe?

She has read the 9/11 truth accounts so many times (and formatted every footnote) that she sometimes finds it hard to recall the so-called official account, or: what really happened. Though she had been twenty that day and remembered it with the clarity you would expect. (The boy had been seven and on the other side of the world.) At one point one of the 9/11 truth books threw some official's account into doubt because he'd claimed he'd watched on TV as first one plane, then the next, hit the towers. Not so, the book had protested: the first crash had not been televised. Of course, she thought, how could it have been? Yet if anyone had asked she might have said she'd seen it too.

When the first plane hit the first tower she was in a college library in Massachusetts, news of the attack spreading in a murmur, not a TV in sight.

*

A current of rage that moved through her: although she cannot join the 9/11 truthers she knows the heat in their words. She has felt it for years; she felt it pervade in New York, February 15, 2003: *No blood for oil*. Around the world millions had predicted what violence would proceed after the towers' fall, the 3,000 murdered, and had cried out against it. The largest protest event in history and it was of no consequence. The war on Iraq commenced. What could anyone have done? What could anyone do now? In time options were reduced to mourning, reconciliation, or vengeance.

The truthers' emotions were right, she thought, just misdirected. Crimes enough had been committed, there was blood enough on American hands, without an elaborate theory that blamed them for the planes. Blame for that particular evil lay elsewhere. It is enough that the official response had been vengeance and greed, shock and awe, mass destruction, this was enough to rage against. Enough to feel that there could not be enough rage.

Every now and then she'd catch herself surprised at the vehemence—fanaticism—of the authors of the 9/11 truth movement. She had to chide herself: if these men and women truly believed that our government had murdered its own civilians as means to implement its foreign policy—how could they keep silent one minute in the face of such a crime? No wonder their passion and relentlessness. No wonder they filled her inbox. Perhaps she envied them. Her heat had found no such direction.

*

To write a novel was not enough. What can literature be a cause of?

*

The spring the marathon was bombed, the military tribunal of the *mastermind of 9/11*, who has been waterboarded 183 times while in US custody, was meant to have begun at last. She is still waiting.

*

You may recall a few words from the essay "'Some People Push Back': On the Justice of Roosting Chickens"—by an ethnic studies professor who was to lose his job—which inspired national furor when it claimed that those killed in the towers

formed a technocratic corps at the very heart of America's global financial empire—the "mighty engine of profit" to which the military dimension of US policy has always been enslaved—and they did so both willingly and knowingly. Recourse to "ignorance" … counts as less than an excuse among this relatively well-educated elite. To the extent that any of them were un-aware of the costs and consequences to others of what they were involved in... it was because of their absolute refusal to see.... If there was a better, more effective, in fact any other way of visiting some penalty befitting their participation upon the little Eichmanns inhabiting the sterile sanctuary of the twin towers, I'd really be interested in hearing about it.

*

Little Eichmanns?

*

She'd become vegetarian at age sixteen after reading her mother's old copy of *Diet for a Small Planet*. At thirty she became vegan. She heard again these tones of passion and fanaticism in the vegan abolitionist movement. Abolitionism: a stance beyond animal rights that opposes any commodification of animal life, seeing it as equivalent to the com-modification of human life that was slavery. As she decides to become vegan she doesn't quite decide about this metaphor. She desires sin-cerely to minimize suffering, to practice compassion for the nonhuman world. At this time she is very ill and can't be politically active otherwise; she thinks that this way she will at least be doing something, there will be something she can do. *First do no harm*—nonviolence as first principle. Perhaps the purity appeals to her; perhaps the sense of control.

Yet she wonders if it's right to conceive of human and animal as equal before the law. Such an argument may paradoxically differentiate them all the more: no other animal debates the morality of its sustenance; no other animal attempts to counter the rhythms of survival and death that are us. And wouldn't any animal in a state of crisis (agree that survival is a continual state of crisis) determine its moral sphere as needed, who was in, who out?

She liked to think that she could choose. That the world could present a moral path and she set forth upon it. But was that what the world was ever doing? And to what facts must compassion answer?

*

One 9/11 truth argument has always especially annoyed her: the claim that the hijackers could not have been zealots, could not have been fanatical enough to sacrifice themselves, because there was evidence that in the days before the attack they'd gotten drunk, gone to a strip club, ordered a lap dance or two. To her this proved only that they were as human as anyone.

ON THE AFTERNOON of September 11, 2001, she sat on the floor of her dorm room, her roommate's TV on, all class and practice canceled. She didn't know what to do. A friend came by and said: Come on, we're going for a run. The friend's father worked in Manhattan but mercifully she had already heard from him; this was during the hours when few calls got through. They ran ten miles in the woods, stopping at one point to take off their shoes and wade across a stream onto some farmland. They saw a couple, the farmers, it seemed, and the four of them greeted each other with uncommon warmth.

Save the phone lines for the dying, a friend who worked a couple blocks from the towers would say as explanation for why she'd been slow to call.

*

The friend she had run with was a woman of unusual empathy. One autumn a bone in her left foot had snapped mid-run and this friend came to feel a pain in her own left foot; the friend said that her whole life she had felt sympathy pains she could not otherwise explain.

In later years they had a falling out and spoke little for some time. A character in her novel bore some relation to this same woman; she did not mention this to her until the novel was published and a copy ready to be mailed. During the years she'd worked on the novel she believed that when the time came the woman would forgive her. Or would think no trespass had been committed.

And this was what occurred. Upon learning a character might resemble her the woman wrote: *If she turns out to be evil, don't worry. I have found plenty of evil in my own heart, so that even on my best day I do not imagine myself to be capable of much good on my own.*

*

The day the war in Iraq began she had been in San Francisco. She was on vacation with the man who would become her first husband; they were visiting a friend who had moved back to the West Coast after graduating. (A friend who would later be diagnosed with both Crohn's disease and multiple sclerosis; those with one autoimmune disease are unfortunately likely to have more than one.) This friend came from a family who, like the city itself, had a history of radicalism, one might say, or simply of political engagement. The parents had been involved with several movements of the sixties and seventies; they were now of course middle-aged, had jobs and adult children, belonged to a commune outside the city they could travel to on weekends, but were still quite active, these days especially in protest of the Israeli occupation of the Palestinian territories.

Good company, then, in which to protest the newest war. The Wednesday bombs began to fall on Baghdad, San Francisco expressed its dissent. Posters everywhere goaded you to call in sick and take to the streets: *No more business as usual*, the day's slogan.

Downtown protestors patiently lay down in intersections and patiently were arrested, plastic-handcuffed and trucked away. As soon as one crossing was cleared protestors were assembling in the next. To her surprise the downtown was home to a number of major corporations (at least two would later be awarded contracts for the reconstruction of Iraq); naively she had always thought of the city in terms of its Beat history and not as an American city like any other, financial center at its heart. They traveled to the protest's stated meeting place and from there departed with a group intending to *storm the federal building.*

The federal building was a complex, really, and took fairly long to march around, but the protestors were many and sufficed to seal it off with their presence. Police came to supervise, though they stood at a distance; across the street the building's workers waited, impassive or on the phone, to see if they would be allowed in. *Go home,* the protesters shouted. *No business. As usual.* Every song and chant was new to her. Her friend's mother, an old hand, passed among the activists who were staking out the building's steps and would be arrested, collecting IDs from those who wished to remain anonymous.

She has often told the story of the *Pukers for Peace*: men dispersed throughout the march chugged gallons of milk dyed red or blue. In the instant before they vomited they'd shout *War makes me sick!* All day while marching she stepped over and around puddles of bright vomit, which stank more with each circumambulation.

*

Her mother has written a book—a work of nonfiction—in which she, the teenage daughter, appears. Although the action of the book takes place during the years of her anorexia, the illness is not mentioned. The book centers on a goose who lived on the pond across from her childhood home. The goose had a broken wing and late one autumn was left alone on the pond after all the flocks had migrated. *Solitary Goose*, her mother called him, and fed him, and worried daily about the approaching winter.

One morning she and her brother were walking in the woods by the pond and heard a distressed honking. As they neared they saw a single goose frozen in the pond's center: the water must have iced over as he slept. They could do nothing; the ice was too thin for even a child to walk upon. Later in the day it warmed enough that he could free himself.

One day the mother summoned her husband, both children, and a few friends, a team of seven armed with sheets and towels and a cat carrier, and running at a stooped shuffle the mother drove the goose toward the others, who with their barriers of fabric steered the bird into the cage. The goose lived out the next few seasons at a wildlife refuge; when his wing was fully healed he was set free.

The mother's book reflects carefully upon the affection and responsibility she felt for the goose: to what degree was she guilty of anthropomorphism? What can two such distinct species perceive of one another? What happens when she tries to speak of, to conjure, the goose within the confines of a foreign language?

But it is not her place to tell the mother's story.

As luck would have it the counselor she eventually saw to treat her anorexia had an office near the wildlife refuge. The mother would drop the daughter off at her session and spend the hour with the solitary goose.

*

But doesn't that theory of anorexia in effect blame the mother? For— the theory suggests—if the mother could only have offered herself as model of balanced and contented womanhood, the daughter may not have sought out the abyss. This implication hardly seems just.

Nothing: a gathering at the house when she was a child—her father's friends from work or tennis, stopping over for a beer, perhaps, or perhaps just the neighbors. The neighborhood kids were in their usual horde in the yard or street then the house, where they discovered her mother upstairs, writing at a lap desk she uses to this day. She may have had a question to ask the mother or the children may just have roamed their way into the bedroom. In any case they would not have been easily persuaded to leave. Suddenly her mother rose and without explanation walked right out of the house, in huge strides down the long driveway to the street, briskly toward the big road. Mornings the girl watched their neighbor power-walk with a Dalmatian along this same route. When she asked her father what was wrong he said: Nothing. She's just going for a walk.

Though such equations are not possible sometimes she imagines the books her mother didn't write in the years she spent caring for her two children. Teaching college courses as an adjunct, working freelance. Her mother's book came out when she was fifty-nine.

She was thirty-one when her first book was published, the age her mother had been when she became a mother.

*

By age thirty her husband had published, extraordinarily, three books of poetry, one of prose. It was not that he had feared he'd die young—that fear had been his father's, who (his mother now confessed) throughout her husband's and his sister's childhood had feared he was fated to die young like the men before him, his own father dead when he was just eleven. And indeed the father did get cancer in his forties, but survived it; fifteen years passed before its return, and he was sixty when he died. They'd known nothing of mutated genes until this recurrence. Her husband had not grown up, then, as his father had, with the fear born of a father's early death. This had come to him only later, only now; and so could not explain the passion with which he wrote through his youth. Or, it could.

*

There were times she could not forgive herself for her illness. Upon divorce from her first husband. Or, in the autumn of 2011, when two hundred miles away a movement suddenly emerged. Its spirit implausibly anarchic, infectious: Occupy Wall Street. That year had already offered the unforeseen vitality of the Arab Spring; for weeks she and a roommate had watched the news, magnetized, and she had felt as if—what?—some specter of herself, a self she didn't know but might be, might somehow be among the masses resolutely claiming Tahrir Square. She was on the couch as always, but could she not feel, even if only through video clips on Al-Jazeera English, something of the force of those men and women, could she not offer them something of the strength that illness had seized from her? She watched.

To think that this power might animate not only streets across the Middle East, where daily with inconceivable courage people faced government snipers, but that this spirit might manifest even here, in the heart of the superpower, the absent shadow of the towers. That there was attention enough to the sufferings of the *Arab world* that Americans could be so moved. Perhaps it was not a question of attention; perhaps these events occurred on some other plane, beyond conscious choice. Transfer of momentum; spontaneous distillation of youth and rage.

The Occupy movement may have refused definition and concrete demands, but it addressed itself to the same empire that sustained the tyrants of the Middle East, from whose rule people now struggled anew to liberate themselves.

Her Facebook feed testified to the encampment's daily speeches, its poetry readings, the burgeoning contents of its library. Her part, it seems, was to read her Facebook feed.

The movement spread nationally, internationally, but not a ripple touched their small town. When she turned away from the news she heard no echo, nothing of these events. Every week at the farmer's market a few unkempt skater boys handed out free slices of cheap cake, handfuls of potato chips, beneath a sign proclaiming *Food not bombs*, but they had nothing to do with anything. She and her husband had moved here a few months before and at first she'd been enamored of the little city, its Victorian rowhouses, its downtown alternately quaint and shabby, half lively and half depressed. But as the fall progressed and she sank further into ill health she came to despise her surroundings.

It can't be fair to say that no one spoke of world events when for so many weeks she was confined and spoke to no one. When other than a few of her husband's colleagues she knew no one there to speak to.

If only she were well, she thought, she could have gone. Taken a train, armed with sleeping bag and backpack, and been welcomed into the

Zeitgeist, the political blossoming of her generation. But would she have? This she didn't know about herself; this was a self illness prevented her from knowing. Would she have joined, had she been able? Or would she still only have watched, perhaps have talked to people, donated food and stacks of books and then gone home to write?

That fall she thought that perhaps she'd gotten everything wrong. Her novel, as yet unpublished, was wrong. She had misunderstood the moment, her own time. She had written in anger and mourning, her novel an elegy to failed hope; but others upon living, witnessing, the same decade had discovered new ground upon which to act. When the war in Iraq had begun she had believed that the fury on the streets of New York and San Francisco would only grow, that this war would prove to be her generation's Vietnam and soon the culture would sunder. (The protests in San Francisco had gone on for days, each day smaller and more ominous, protestors matched in number by police, instead of chants and singing only shouting or wordless drumming one could hear for blocks.) But this did not occur, a disappointment—betrayal—she'd had to write a book to try to comprehend. Each morning as it sent its children off to war in two countries, her nation tongued its forefinger and turned past the front page, finished its coffee and arose to go on with, as they say, *business as usual*.

Later she would feel nostalgic even for this disappointment, this incredulity: for the young woman who'd had hope enough to mourn its defeat.

And now—Occupy. Not a protest, quite; not vengeance. Mourning? Reconciliation? Not a political movement in that it refused to articulate a political agenda, refused the discourse of routine governance. But perhaps in that refusal and in the reclamation of public space, where a communal, anti-capitalist practice of daily living may take place in the city's heart—perhaps in this performance of values there was mourning for what had been done, what had not been lived, there was hope for a nation that might yet exist, or which existed momentarily here. She had in the past decade failed to sustain such thoughts; she had known her dreams of action as mere dreams. Had she been wrong? Now that there was this *assertion of social optimism*, this *triumph over grim context*? Hope had not failed; she had failed hope—this the sort of thought she had that fall.

Is a dream of action *merely* a dream?

Could the suffering of years of occupation—Afghanistan, Iraq—be transformed into the hope of Occupy?

And now, years later, was Occupy itself mere dream, a haunting of the agora?

She did not know what she would have felt nor come to believe had she too slept in those streets, offered her face to pepper spray and her voice to the crowd, the possibilities of unison. She might simply have returned to her desk, which is where each day so far had brought her; each day the illness broke, there she was again. It seems this practice—a woman daily at her desk, writing—was the form her hope assumed. Was this its limit?

Perhaps her exchange of hope for mourning and rage had been merely personal. Each year she grew sicker. In those days she often had occasion to wonder: if this continued to be the *progress* of the illness, what life would be left to her? What measure of time? She might consider these questions practically. She could still manage to write if she were only well enough one day out of two, or two weeks wrested out of any month. But when it was just one day in three, one in four. When it was none. What would be possible? Who would she become?

That fall she feared the book she'd written would be the last one, and after it she would endure decades of silence.

Reduced to onlooker, disabled—was she now one of those on the margins for whom movements claim to speak? Those *who cannot speak for themselves*. Those who cannot work, who are denied health-care (though, through good fortune, marriage, graduate school, she had never gone without). She did not feel at home in that battle cry: *we are the 99 percent*. She felt at once too fortunate and too alone.

Why wouldn't they just say something? Someone, anyone among them? she thought increasingly. When they had the platform, why not use it? Who would choose silence when they could still speak?

*

Back in Kyrgyzstan the brothers' father had been an attorney and worked for the government; or this was a story he told. During a purge he claims he was jailed and beaten. In the US he worked as a car mechanic, unlicensed. One article notes that

his behavior was sometimes erratic—perhaps because he was suffer-ing from post-traumatic stress disorder that he attributed to his mal-treatment back in Kyrgyzstan. He received psychiatric therapy... and suffered from severe headaches and intense abdominal pain (probably psychosomatic in origin, since doctors were unable to find the cause).

*

And why suggest kinship or rhyme between *occupying* Iraq and *occupying* Wall Street? Even those dreamers, arrested daily, presenting themselves to parks and streets and plastic handcuffs nationwide: they became occupiers because they already were.

*

She might have fallen in love with her first husband because he had left. One morning in college (*that country club*, he called it), he had packed a bag and, roommate still asleep, he was gone, hitchhiking across the country, sleeping in the bed of a pickup to awake to dawn in Arizona. His friends, family, various administrators were stunned; some time passed before they heard from him. His internet history offered only a wink: a map of the US, star in its center. The seduction of this rupture; she was seduced. Later he returned; later they were married. They had a dog and three chessboards. He became an attorney. Her departure from the marriage was less sudden, though it too was, she was told, unexpected. She didn't return.

AFTER THE LATEST of ceaseless officials had harassed him for vending without a permit, a fruit seller had bought a can of gasoline, walked to the local government office, doused himself and lit a match. He's said first to have cried out to the traffic: *How do you expect me to make a living?*

Within a month his nation had arisen and overthrown its corrupt dictatorship. The revolution spread—Egypt, Libya, Yemen, Bahrain, Syria, and beyond—and his name and story were everywhere. By which time he had died of his injuries.

*

The layman's explanation of Crohn's disease is as you'd expect: the immune system, usually our defense against *foreign invaders*, instead begins to attack *harmless bacteria, many of which aid in digestion*. In the body this state of endless warfare is chronic inflammation.

Recent research alters the story's emphasis. It's not that some bacteria are harmless, but that they are necessary: the life we know as human, the bodies we live in, not only rely upon but are inseparable from them. Those with Crohn's disease have been found to have less diverse bacteria than those with healthy guts; they have *the wrong mix*. Here the enemy is hard to distinguish; the enemy melts back into the crowd.

*

The centrality of detail, detail become clue: while she agrees in theory with this explication of detective fiction, this is not how she reads. When to pass the long dull days she immerses herself in mystery she does not wish to *solve*. Nor is her weakened style of reading suited for attending to detail—she often misses items of significance and upon reaching the novel's end has to flip back to seek clues out. In any case she would never wish to diminish her pleasure by knowing the solution before it's given. When she can't help but figure it out she's quite disappointed. It's as if she reads with a deliberate disregard for any detail that might signify. Desiring mystery, not solution.

*

Consider how they discovered the man and the boy. Among the thousands of surveillance-camera images—most of the cameras privately owned—of that time and place were two in which the brothers and their backpacks appeared. Within three days their faces were on screens around the world. Later that same day, one would be dead.

*

The older brother was known to read the English-language al-Qaeda–affiliated magazine *Inspire*. Articles report that he built the bombs by following instructions the magazine supplied; articles contest this claim, noting the *sophistication* of the brothers' *switch/ trigger*. A photo: gruesomely blood-stained pavement in which elements of the bomb are embedded, a ruler beside them for scale.

Inspire was published by an American citizen, a young man of Pakistani descent who grew up in Queens. He left the US for Yemen, where he joined a fundamentalist cleric who was also American and who became an editor of the magazine. It was in Yemen that in 2011 both he and the cleric were assassinated by American drone.

Not until 2013—though it had been common knowledge—did the US government formally admit that it had targeted and killed the cleric and, as though incidentally, the men with him. Two weeks after the assassination of the cleric, the cleric's son—sixteen years old, American—was also killed in a drone strike by his own government. When a journalist questioned one US official about the murder of the child, the official said stumblingly something about *bad parenting*: how if the boy's father had wanted to keep his son safe he would not have chosen the path of violent jihad.

Though its publisher and editor are dead, the magazine continues to publish.

*

In English the poem might begin: *Who, if I cried out, would hear me among the orders of angels?*

*

In the United States suicide increased significantly during and after what is known as the Great Recession: from 2007 to 2010 there were 4,750 more suicides than would have been predicted; or 4,750 *excess suicides*.

Since the economic crisis in Greece and the advent of austerity policies, infant mortality has risen 40 percent; new HIV infections have more than doubled.

Studies note that in nations that suffered economic crisis but did not implement austerity, public health has shown no significant ill effects.

Experts conclude: unemployment is a pandemic. Austerity kills.

*

Did the official slap the fruit seller, as reports claim? Some disagree; others add that she then spat upon him. Did the fact that she was a woman contribute to his sudden despair? Or perhaps lifelong poverty in a corrupt state sufficed to humiliate him, to humiliate anyone.

*

Of late her favorite works of detective fiction do not center on the clue. They conclude not with the triumph of logic but the defeat of self-deception. The solution has been obvious, we come to realize; the mystery lay in our unwillingness to admit to its truth.

In one recent novel, for example: an entire family has been brutally slain, even two small children. The family was on that verge of middle class breaking into upper middle; they lived in one of the luxury housing developments that Ireland built to excess throughout its boom years. Upon the advent of the Great Recession it is as though everywhere the money has evaporated. The development stands nearly empty, its cheaply built houses falling into decay; the family loses its grip on rung after rung of the socioeconomic ladder it had ascended; a new and nightmarish poverty looms. But who then attacks them? The novel answers this question; the answer resonates not because of the ability, the logic, employed to discover it, but for the opposite reason, or the opposite of reason: we did not wish, truly, to know, or we'd have known many pages ago. The sleuth shares our blindness; with him we learn to see.

Another novel, this one from Scotland, works similarly: in this case the reader knows more than the sleuth throughout; the narrator is, we think, on our side. Throughout we believe we know who committed the crime; the suspense is in watching the sleuth catch up, clue by clue. But at the last minute we see how wrong we were, how we'd pinned the guilt on the wrong boy. For this there was, we must confess, no excuse, except that among the characters before us we loved this boy more; we had desired a different story, a different truth, in which those for whom we feel compassion would not fail us.

A contemporary mode of detective fiction: the clue is not the means by which one may *triumph over grim context*, no means to *optimism*. The clue, in its merciless facticity, confirms the grimness of that context; the clue forces us fools, all those less clear-eyed than the sleuth, to abandon our irrational optimism. Here justice is hard to recognize.

*

American readers have little appetite for foreign literature, but for mysteries they make an exception. Note the recent popularity of Scandinavian crime novels. In a Swedish novel she just read, the sleuth had to come to terms with the speed of change in his native land, the *decay of social institutions*, one might say; and to the American reader this may seem an appealing anachronism. We have lived for decades in Chandler's Los Angeles, fallen irredeemably, its dream corrupted from its very conception. That there are places one might experience corruption in the present tense—how novel. To the Swedish city in the novel even immigration from the so-called Third World was new.

Americans still want to believe that through globalization the world may become, should become, everywhere more American. That we recognize the potential Americanness of others makes us more proudly American.

How white Americans call themselves Irish or Scottish or Italian or—any hyphenated self that offers authenticity, an emphasis on the *American* with which the compound concludes.

Perhaps it is the appeal of (exaggerated?) heritage that inclines Americans to crime novels from Ireland and Scotland, from Scandinavia, etc. Or, these novels may serve as another means by which Americans read their own empire. Isn't there a quaintness, are these lands not so small, so contained? So powerless? The Irish and Scottish subjugated by the last empire, not our own, so that one may allow oneself the pleasure of feeling allied with them. These places are no threat, their crimes an entertainment from the hinterlands. If there are rends in their social fabric, this may seem merely the fraying of curtains upon a favored stage.

*

Photographs from the finish line show a man, bearded and wearing a cowboy hat, disappearing into the smoke. Later the man, still with cowboy hat, is seen bent over a man in a wheelchair, pinching closed an artery in the man's bloodied leg. The man in the cowboy hat was there to cheer for a group of military servicemen who were marching the course in honor of fallen soldiers, including the man in the cowboy hat's son, killed in Najaf in 2004. The servicemen marched in full uniform and bore forty-pound rucks, their efforts dedicated not only to those who had died in combat but those lost to suicide upon their return.

When in 2004 three marines came to tell the man in the cowboy hat of his son's death, he could not believe them, and in his grief he doused the marines' van in gasoline, from within set it on fire, set himself on fire. Later he traveled around the country to protest the war and the military's recruitment practices, which he believed had been intended to deceive his son. *As long as there are marines fighting and dying in Iraq, I'm going to share my mourning with the American people*, he told a reporter, interviewed beside a coffin he had transformed into traveling memorial.

P.S. Please send some info. about Afghanistan, Saudi Arabia, Iran, Iraq. We get very little amounts of info. down here…. But I have heard some little things here and there about Conflicts, War, Deployments, etc., his son wrote from boot camp in 2002.

From Iraq his son wrote, *We go out every day with the police and do what a beat cop does, patrol the streets. We mostly just deal with shootings and robberies.*

P.S. Oh yeah, the cops are teaching me Arabic.

In 2011 the soldier's brother—the man in the cowboy hat's younger son—committed suicide. He had suffered from depression, his family said, since his brother's death.

The injured man in the photograph, pale and ash-smeared in the wheelchair, would lose both legs but survive.

The military servicemen may be seen in photographs, wrenching a fence clear of the blast scene, trying to get to those injured within.

WHEN THE SURGEONS send her husband home they say his new digestive system—colon removed—will take a few weeks to get used to. When she and her husband talk to others who have had this surgery—when her husband, up late in pain, skims online forums—they say it takes a year.

Throughout his recovery her schedule is quite open. She has been healthy for two months now, but since she had been sick for years before this, she doesn't have much of a job to return to. She writes every morning, then wonders at the expanse of the afternoon. Her husband spends most of these first weeks in her former position: propped up on pillows watching TV on his laptop. He prefers comedy to mystery. The cramping is intermittent and extremely painful.

It is no easy thing to sit at her desk and write while he is suffering. But there is no relief to offer; and who benefits from sympathy pains?

Sometimes what is not easy is how easy it is, in fact, to sit and write, as though without regard for his condition.

For twelve years she is ill, and the man who loves her must depart each morning, leaving her in bed alone and to a day of uselessness, despair. Must hoist her up by her elbows and torso when she has buckled again to the floor. When her spine in that dumb habit twitches and her limbs spasm. When absurdly she collapses just as he tries to embrace her. As she stands, for instance, at the stove. It is one of her few tasks each day, to cook dinner, a means to feel useful, the hour she anticipates through the long afternoon, when he will come home and say something of his day, the world she hasn't seen, and she will have done one thing—made the meal before them, which she eats each night too quickly—and she will repeat perhaps one thing she read online, as though this represented her day.

She has known this was a trial to witness; she knows there is suffering in the observance of suffering. But until now that knowledge has been intellectual or ethical: a nod to justice. That she ought to acknowledge the suffering she in her illness causes. But she understood this never so well as in those weeks after his surgery, when in her study she could hear his moaning from the bedroom, where he lay upon his side at an angle that exposed his new skinniness.

She could not pay off the debt, if debt there is. She goes to the grocery store, as he had always done for them. She gets him every kind of coffee ice cream and barbecue potato chips, and is grateful.

*

The man in the cowboy hat is from Costa Rica. If his son had died two months later, a new law would have granted the father US citizenship, in honor of—in exchange for?—his child's sacrifice.

*

Some doctors had called her illness *chronic fatigue syndrome*, a diagnosis others would later rescind. One nurse went so far as to erase the words from her chart. There was a stigma to this diagnosis: you may recall that this disease was once known as the *yuppie flu*.

*

Two decades after the first Gulf War, a study concludes that Gulf War Syndrome is *fundamentally biological in nature*. Doctors had argued it was psychological; but MRIs attest to real damage in sufferers' brains. Some remain skeptical; one professor notes that it's not that he questions the reality of the symptoms, he questions *whether these symptoms have any cause other than the stress of war*.

*

That she expected the war in Iraq to be to her generation what Vietnam was to her parents'. Has she once more mistaken the private for the public? Does she mean the personal for the political? What can she know of her parents' generation—when she speaks of the war, does she mean only their war, mean only them?

Even five decades later her mother curses McNamara and Kissinger.

Her mother hopping off her exercise bicycle whenever President Reagan appeared on TV—a political ad; a disaster great enough to interrupt daytime soaps—to fetch two styrofoam rocks she kept handy to hurl at his face onscreen.

Her father's birthday had been the third date called out on the first night of the draft. He had not served: he had, and this she thinks was his phrase, *thrown some bad physicals*. As a student he had been in ROTC—for some years his uniform hung in their garage, awaiting what fate—and so he could not qualify as a conscientious objector. So he had dieted, lost enough weight to call himself into question.

After the war he lost weight again and dramatically, but this time had no choice: he suffered from ulcerative colitis. Doctors told him he had a *colitic personality*. He spent months in the hospital and after long illness his colon was removed. She has been told that after the surgery her father's father said to her mother, *You saved his life*. He believed that without her his son would not have survived the ordeal and its recovery. She herself never heard her grandfather say anything sentimental, and perhaps that is why this statement has entered their family lore.

The war in Vietnam: a thatched roof set deliberately alight. A young man with an Afro smokes and speaks into the camera and when it pans out we see he has no legs. You too may have seen this film, a documentary called *Hearts and Minds*. How else could she picture a war that ended years before her birth? The years her parents spent in protest bequeath no image as vivid.

Four decades after the war ends her father goes to Vietnam. He is there to train students of library science in the use of information technology. He finds that an etiquette exists to greet American men of his generation: *Is this your first visit?*

*

After dinner, a few glasses of wine, her husband's parents would chuckle at how in the seventies their professors encouraged them to drop out of school. Drop out they did; the professors kept their jobs. His parents lived here and there, baked bread to sell, worked jobs they collapse into laughter to describe now. Eventually the father went back to finish his bachelor's. When their first child, her husband's sister, was born severely disabled, he got a job in state government; she cared full time for their girl. Now, four decades later, mother and daughter live on his savings, state pensions, and Social Security.

*

Four months before the marathon was bombed, a young man— twenty, a year older than the younger of the brothers—had taken guns from the home where he lived with his mother, shot his mother to death, then walked to a local elementary school. There he killed twenty children and six adults; when first responders arrived he killed himself. According to Wikipedia, this was the second deadliest mass shooting in American history and the second deadliest mass murder at an American elementary school.

She understands the meaning of *second deadliest* but still pauses. In death isn't there only one degree?

Upon hearing the sound of gunfire or the word *shooter*—over the loudspeaker? from the custodian who ran shouting warnings through the halls?—teachers hid their students in closets, bathrooms, under desks, or behind their own bodies.

In the two days after the marathon bombing, the Senate failed to pass two gun-control measures put forward as response to the winter's school shooting. One bill would have banned high-capacity magazines, which the boy had used against children in the school and which many fellow mass shooters had used in recent atrocities. One bill would have expanded background checks for gun purchases, a measure that some 90 percent of Americans support. Such checks would not have kept this particular boy from access to the guns his mother purchased; nor would it have prevented Boston's two bombers from buying the guns they used to murder one campus law-enforcement officer and then in a shootout with police, since at least the younger brother had no record.

But most of the 33,000-plus gun-related deaths that occur each year in the US are neither top news stories nor such public spectacles. 21,000 of them are suicides.

In 2010, there were 31,672 deaths caused by gunfire in the US. In Ireland there were 43. Sweden, 138. The United Kingdom, 165. A magnitude of difference cop shows and detective fiction tend not to reveal.

The *typical victims* of a gun homicide are neither children nor law-enforcement officers nor, for that matter, marathoners and their fans. Heavily over-represented among the dead are young black and Latino men; whites are under-represented. 78 percent of victims, and 89 percent of offenders, are male.

*

Upon hearing the word *Chechnya* you may think of a school,

perhaps an image like: a man in military uniform carries a blood-ied child in his arms, backdrop of smoke. On September 1, 2004, first day of the school year, thirty-two militants entered a school in North Ossetia, neighbor to Chechnya. Central among their demands: for Chechnya's independence to be recognized, for Russian troops to withdraw from the would-be state. For 53 hours the militants held over 1,100 men, women, and children hostage; in the end 331 of the hostages would be dead. The hostages were held in the gym, imprisoned at gunpoint and by an arrangement of bombs and cables. The bombs detonated; Russian forces stormed the school; a gunfight commenced. This series of events is still contested.

After the siege many doubted the government's account and believed that opportunities for negotiation with the militants had been deliberately wasted, the tragedy exploited as occasion to further consolidate Russian power. Recall that tanks had fired on the school while hostages were still within. The government forces used flamethrowers, a weapon that cannot, as one commentator has noted, be used *surgically*. Evidence has been presented that the bombs were set off by Russian fire; if so, this would mean most of the hostages had been killed indirectly by authorities and not by the terrorists. Many mothers of the dead fear this is true.

*

Some mothers go further, and say things like: *I don't doubt that the whole thing was ordered by Moscow.*

*

Here in the US some claim that the shooting in the elementary school was perpetrated by government forces, to be used as pretense for new gun-control laws. Some say the whole massacre was a hoax, the parents of the slain children *crisis actors*.

As for the marathon bombing, the government was behind that too. Or the Saudis were. Or—and they're to blame for the school shooting as well—the Israelis, or just say the Jews.

*

Is her love of detective fiction due to *nature* or *nurture*? When she was a girl she read everything on her mother's shelves: Conan Doyle, Christie, Sayers, Peter Dickinson, Josephine Tey. When she read

Tey's novel on Richard III—did he or didn't he kill the two princes?—her mother tried to interest her in the history; she drifted back toward the novels. Her mother supplied her with other books too, books her mother loved, books with which a young woman could improve her mind: *Jane Eyre, Emma, The Diary of Anne Frank, My Brilliant Career.* She may or may not have read them then; she has read them now. As a girl she was always reading and would have to be goaded into joining the family for a walk in the woods, or getting ready for swim practice, though she knew it was time.

She knew she ought to read more serious books, and sometimes she did, though mostly she read what she wished and felt guilty.

Summers she was sick in her twenties she might spend a few weeks in her parents' house while they traveled, caring for the two dogs, theirs and hers. The weeks passed slowly: she'd awake in illness and walk the dogs, feeling already the jittery weakness that would soon claim the day. She walked the dogs up the hill to the overgrown trails of a nearby park, which the highway skimmed over at a roar, and where one might see a few other dog walkers she'd have to restrain her dog from, or someone's sleeping bag, or young men playing paintball or riding ATVs, or no one. Her parents would fill bags with littered bottles as they walked; she did not. She felt guilty that she was too ill to walk the dogs again later: she'd summon herself for a quick around-the-block or would sit in a chair in the yard in the sun and throw a ball for her parents' dog, who never tired. She insisted that after fetching he drop the ball, heavy with spit, precisely where she could reach it so she wouldn't have to waste herself getting up. The dog's expression never changed. Her own dog, more like her, amused himself playing with a large rock, or just lying down in a hole he'd dug in the shade. Those weeks she fed herself on frozen foods she didn't eat otherwise and her parents' decadent organic breakfast cereals. She was not what anyone would call happy, though she might have felt useful, since in her illness she at least had a task: to care for two animals. No, three: there was a cat, who preferred solitude and whom she saw rarely. She was alone and saw few people those weeks, and she knows that this occurred several summers, but was it now possible to know which ones? What to do with the days? Unwell she returned to the shelves of detective fiction she'd fed upon as an adolescent, ten, twelve, fourteen years before. She reread; she read all her mother had in the intervening years acquired. She lay on her parents' bed and watched endless episodes of *Law & Order*. Her mother had many shows recorded on

VHS, made in the years before there existed entire channels evidently just to broadcast reruns of *Law & Order*. From the opening scene of the murdered corpse, even before the credits—the jingle you can now recall—her mother can say who did it and what the issue at trial will be. Not through powers of deduction, of course, but memory.

When she was a girl and her family had watched TV or a movie while eating dinner, she would many nights get up mid-plot and slip away. Not to read, but to pace in her room or outside in a sort of daydreaming in which she must by now have spent years but does not know how to name. To have had so little appetite for TV then, and now to find herself out of necessity *glued to the screen*.

Her dreams now peopled by TV characters. Her ideas of how people might speak to one another, of what a city might be. She speaks to herself—an old bad habit the other dog walkers may catch her in—and lives not in a city but in a bedroom, a kitchen, on a couch, a chair in a yard. Online.

In recent years technology allows her to watch almost any show, any film, at any time. Her mother's old videotapes, labeled by season, lose all value, except as trace of a gesture, a laying in of stores. This new wealth is a gift to the sick, although a gift for which she wishes she had not had years of occasions to feel grateful. Still she is dissatisfied; she cannot choose among the thousands of movies and shows she could view, since what she wants is a life in which she does not watch television two to ten hours a day. She watches detective shows. If there's a series, then she can hit *next episode* and needn't make another choice. The rhythm appeals: the show begins with a crime, proceeds to a resolution. Next episode.

When she visits her parents' house now she often finds that her mother has a detective show playing continually in some room somewhere, background to whatever task, to the passing hours.

How many murders is it that the average American will have seen on TV, by what age? Fewer than occur here each year, surely, though that should be no consolation.

She feels guilty about the shows. Although her body, no, also her brain—the illness is, after all, neurological—have retreated from the world, shouldn't she resist, find what world she can? Rather

than numbing herself. But what if one needs such anesthesia? No—
she ought to wring whatever use she can from these lost days, learn
something, occupy herself with, say, one thought. One thought a day.
Some redemption for the dark stagnant hours, something she might
say, might write of, might answer to, later, when health returns for a
day here, a morning there. A better person—a better writer—would
resist; would still be present somehow in the world; would use this
time, no, *use* was the wrong word. Who was this better person? She
wishes she knew her, could talk to her. What anyone else does with
their years of illness she doesn't know. Despite whatever blog.

She queues up dozens of documentaries she might watch, learn
something (*your genocide docos*, her husband calls them; genocide is
somehow a common theme). She does watch them. She watches, for
instance, *Hearts and Minds*. She watches a film on Agent Orange, a
film on nonviolent resistance in a Palestinian village, a film on the
Weather Underground, a film or two on the prison in Guantanamo.
Sometimes, though, she chooses one, hits play and can't stand more
than five minutes: there's something sickening to the mechanisms
of the genre, the background music, overly literal graphics, ear-
nest parade of well-labeled talking heads. In contrast the genre of

mystery never exhausts itself: the body, the wisecrack, the bulletin board where faces of interest are pinned.

Sometimes the shows' violence disturbs her; she tries to avoid serial killers, which is harder than you might think. What difference to or in the viewer between a nonfictional representation of real violence (genocide doco) and a fictive representation of imagined violence (her crime shows)? Someone somewhere must be doing a functional MRI to answer this question. Eleven years into her illness she begins seeing a therapist, to cope with the *stress of chronic illness*. She does this for herself but also for her husband, since she has recognized that those weeks in which he is the only one she speaks to may be a burden. Her therapist encourages her to stick to her shows. Those shows are soothing—they begin with a crime and proceed to a resolution, the therapist says, or some phrase so similar to the one she would use that she is taken aback. It's important, the therapist says (and now who could know her exact words), to stay calm, not to upset yourself. There is real care in this perspective, some relief from the guilt she is prone to feel. But still she wonders about *improving her mind*. This is not really a therapist's task—to educate, intellectually, spiritually? Mr. Knightley to her Emma?—so perhaps it should remain her own. Perhaps she might yet, despite everything said, devote her suffering to some cause. If in witnessing representations of real suffering she might cultivate, for example, a deeper compassion. Or would this just be masochism; or a pornography of violence. Is it truly more important to care for herself than to attend to the world in its excess, its horrors? Who is not defeated by such questions, who could even say what she means by *herself* or *world*? A woman, a highway, morning light through leaves, daily fear, a ball she threw too deep in the woods where the dog may not find it.

*

They have moved; they live in Philadelphia. Their house is the nicest either has, as an adult, lived in, and in the first few weeks they rarely leave it, they wander its rooms in a sweet sort of daze, sequestering themselves to write, sitting on a small patio and watching birds feed in the lengthening grass. One night, eve of the year's longest day, they are driving back from seeing friends and he tells her, an apology for having wished to leave just after ten, how fragile he feels. Vulnerable and easily tired. He is still healing, she says, it has been just two months. The scar is raised red flesh beneath her fingers. Since he did nothing to cause the cancer, he can do nothing to assure it will not return. Something in the body may already be failing, something monstrous may already be flourishing. There is only vigilance and for this they must entrust themselves to others' theories, others' hands.

For years she relied on a test to tell her what kind of day she was to have, whether a late morning's fatigue or quick irritation was in fact prologue to illness. Push-ups. As illness approaches and strength recedes, she can't do even one. She'll lower herself and be stuck there, face pressed to carpet or linoleum, laughing. There goes the day. She has been healthy for four months now; every day or two she drops to the floor to try the old test: ten push-ups to tell herself that nothing is wrong.

*

Please don't let them be Muslim, commentators wrote in the short days between bombing and manhunt. She sympathized, but the wishfulness annoyed. Why shouldn't they be Muslim, given the violence the US had perpetrated for decades across the Muslim world? Long-standing support for the Israeli occupation of Palestine, wars waged in Iraq and Afghanistan, drone strikes in Pakistan, Yemen, and elsewhere, long-standing support for dictators across the region, only a few of them now overthrown.

The US army psychiatrist who in 2009 killed thirteen and wounded thirty at Fort Hood in a *shooting rampage* was Muslim. He was about to be deployed to one of America's two war zones; the soldiers he attacked were in a processing center to be vaccinated before being sent overseas. A first responder shot the psychiatrist four times; he survived, paralyzed from the chest down.

At his trial, set to begin this summer, he will represent himself. He argues that his actions were a *defense of others*: in his assault he acted to defend the leaders of the Taliban from American forces. The judge will not allow this defense.

*

In 2012 an army veteran killed six and wounded four in a shooting at a Sikh temple. He was shot by a police officer, then shot himself. He was active in what's known as the white-power music scene and *had ties* to white supremacists and neo-Nazis. His bands: End Apathy and Definite Hate. He used a high-capacity magazine; he spoke of *racial holy war*. He had been a psy ops specialist. It is not known why he chose the Sikh temple as target. Upon hearing the news of the attack many had, like her, recalled how in the months after September 11 Sikhs across the country had been attacked: their attackers seemingly thought that Sikhs are Muslim, or couldn't be bothered to make distinctions.

Attacks on American Muslims were, of course, in those same months widespread.

*

Intelligence agencies had intercepted some ten to twenty messages between the psychiatrist—who would soon be *the shooter*—and the cleric in Yemen the US would later kill by drone. Those who have read the correspondence deem it innocuous.

After the murders at Fort Hood, the cleric would say of the psychiatrist: *He is a man of conscience who could not bear the contradiction of being a Muslim and fighting against his own people.*

Both cleric and psychiatrist were born in the US; both had received advanced degrees here. In the months just after September 11 the cleric had been praised as a moderate, sought out as one who might bridge the abyss between *us* and *them*. One journalist notes that it was not until the US invaded Iraq that the cleric became more critical of his government and its policy; it was not until he was, at the behest of his own government, imprisoned in Yemen—seventeen months in solitary confinement—that he became what anyone might call extreme.

Also true, discovered later: three of the nineteen hijackers had attended mosques where the cleric preached and had met with him; the psychiatrist, too, had prayed at a mosque where he served as imam. Yet the evidence indicates they did not speak of violence.

The cleric's great strength as leader, or as propagandist: he was fluent, eloquent, in English. His writings and sermons online drew a following of young men in the US, the UK, worldwide. It was this fluency that had drawn US news outlets and government officials to him after the attacks and before the wars; they could see in him the moderate they desired.

In 2002 the cleric published an essay in praise of suicide bombers: *Why Muslims Love Death*.

He has been *linked to* the hijackers, *linked to* the underwear bomber, *linked to* the psychiatrist, *linked to* the cargo plane plot, *linked to* the

Times Square bomber, although no one knows if they met. His sermons appear in the search histories of so many violent young men. To judge the cleric one must know when inspiration has become operation, when or if speech became act.

Some would say one must have evidence. Though perhaps theories of contagion will do: if so many young men credit him as inspiration, incitement, does their guilt infect him? Or could he have been the source of the disease that transformed each from boy to terrorist?

It is a question of *contact with*.

He preached at the Capitol, attended a breakfast with Pentagon officials.

To what degree, commentators may now ask, was he American? Can one measure nationality by degree? By drop of blood?

Of the four Americans killed by American drones, it seems he was the only one deliberately targeted. He was never charged, never indicted.

Before he lost both his son and grandson, the cleric's father had filed suit in US courts to challenge the government's plans, already widely suspected, to kill his son. The suit was dismissed.

His grandson, sixteen, would die in a strike that according to US officials was meant for an Egyptian al-Qaeda operative; the drone hit a group of friends barbecuing outside, the boy among them. The Egyptian was not there, the boy there only because weeks before he had slipped out of his home in another city, left a note for his mother: *I am going to look for my father.*

*

Fifteen years earlier the cleric, who preached widely against vice and sin, had twice been arrested for soliciting prostitutes. Does this make him more sympathetic or less?

*

But when I say that to judge the cleric *one must know, one must have—* why this use of the modal? All this has been judged. Decisions made, drones dispatched. Now our disputations are no more than, as it were, picking over the bones of history.

*

She finds the cleric's lectures on Youtube; they have fewer views than she'd expected. His accent is indeed American. The audience before him in the clip is all men. This should not surprise her, but she has rarely seen so large a room full of men, not a woman in sight. She is not surprised that she does not find him charismatic, though that is how he has been described. She is surprised that in a brief discourse on the era of US Prohibition, he gets the basic facts quite wrong.

(She is attuned to such matters, having recently watched the TV series *Boardwalk Empire*.)

*

After the marathon bombing, after this or that mass shooting, a chorus arises: why do we mourn those innocents felled in Boston but not those in Baghdad, in Homs? The white children lost to a school shooting, yet not the black children lost to everyday gun violence?

Spectacle: how unexpected a target, the marathon. How pure the shock at the first bomb. The drama—imagine the TV movie; you have practically seen it—of the lone gunman entering the elementary school. Where violence seems foreign its intrusion is so conspicuous, the tragedy almost reassuringly Manichean.

This is no defense; yet it is real, the desire for spectacle. An object for vision to consume, be consumed by. She among the millions that day watching CNN as a city gutted itself in the hunt for a boy.

Or: a square fills with protestors, chanting, kerchiefs pulled up over mouths, tear gas clouds the scene, tanks array themselves around the crowd, and—as if succumbing to the logic of a dream—a dictator yields.

*

Or: the word *cancer*. Which commands from every corner attention; the most uncongenial coworker will sign the card.

When she has had to explain her own illness, she begins *it's like…* She names the episodes *complex migraine*, *atypical migraine*, phrases doctors have used often enough, sometimes assuredly. It is not that the word *migraine* is wrong; rather that it will always be misunderstood. Most who suffer migraine are not disabled as she is; their symptoms are not like hers, hers not like theirs. The devastating headache, which her mother suffers (which she would, if one could select one's inheritances, have preferred). Most who inquire after her health ask, how are your headaches? She has never had headaches, or rather, they are nothing compared to the neurological quagmire. Yet she too will now say: *I have a headache*. Absent a diagnosis, one ends up with a lie.

Although each doctor has in his or her way addressed the complexity of her diagnosis, not one has ever spoken to this point: what name should she offer to others, to the world, if her illness has none? This is beyond the sphere of their concerns; or perhaps the fact of this dilemma has not occurred to them. When she has needed to offer an explanation—one winter she plummeted into illness and had to withdraw from a semester of college—the note from her doctor said only: *She is completely disabled at this time*.

*

It cannot surprise you to learn that the brothers downloaded material by that same cleric. In interrogation the boy is said to have named the cleric as influence, or inspiration, or—she does not know what word he chose.

*

Of course, that cry for justice—*the dead in Boston, yet not in Homs*—itself becomes spectacle. Predictable stage of the civic immune response: to condemn the limits of others' perceptions, find others guilty. To affirm oneself as one who possesses the right sentiment. Hit refresh; repeat.

The dead in Homs, the dead in Boston, were not sacrificed that we might prove our compassion. Yet this is one use to which they may be put. In this sense a foreign body possesses more value. In this sense.

If the one who detonates the bomb is a soldier, our compassion extends to him. If the one who detonates the bomb is a Muslim, an Arab, or the boy, we may require his sacrifice. Our compassion may manifest in his death; if we have named him *terrorist*, he may fulfill this name with his death. If he lives we will not see him; we will see him only by the light of his orange jumpsuit. If he insists on living, or dying, to spite us. If he insists on living in the grave.

*

Some calculate that an American's chances of being killed by an act of terrorism are one in twenty million. Car accident, one in nineteen thousand. A recent statistic attests that more Americans have now died of gun violence than in all the wars of their history combined.

*

Obviously, tonight there are many unanswered questions, the president addressed the nation. *Among them, why did young men who grew up and studied here, part of our communities and country, resort to such violence?*

*

There are places no history can reach

She might begin with this, a line by a writer her mother despises, only to try to disprove it.

THIS LINE SERVES as epigraph to a well-known poem, a poem in which a man *as though balanced / astride the whiplash between system and system* stands outside the Pentagon and sets himself alight.

In 1965, the year he died, the man was the age she is now. He brought his infant daughter with him to the scene of his sacrifice, but she was not harmed. To his wife he sent a letter: *Know that I love thee, but I must act for the children of the priest's village.*

The priest was a stranger, foreigner, a man he had read of in the news: *I have seen my faithful burned up in napalm.*

I should have said: there are two well-known poems. One in English, which she read in college. One in Vietnamese, a poem honoring the man's daughter, which is said to have been popularly recited.

In the poem she knows, the man carries the gasoline to the Pentagon in a wine jug. She does not confirm this fact, since she would like to believe it. The poet does not mention the daughter. In the poem the only children are touched by napalm: *pomegranates of jellied gasoline / that run along the ground, that cling / in a blazing second skin / to the skins of children.*

*

When does a spectacle cease to be? Lose the distinction of that name? In the past four years one hundred and twenty Tibetans have immolated themselves to protest Chinese occupation and oppression. This is little known, little noted, in what is known as the West.

*

The poet published her first major book at age sixty-three.

*

What can literature be a cause of? She stole the question from her husband. Or rather, she has heard him, once or twice in a lecture, ask this, a means for the students before him to think about *the poem as cause not effect*. She is not a student but she still cannot answer the question.

*

This would not be the war we fought in, another poet wrote, forty years ago, in the first year of the draft that did not claim her father. *But I find it impossible not to look for actual persons known / to me and not seen since; impossible not to look for myself.*

*

A woman she barely knows writes her from amid the protests in Istanbul. The protests began when a favorite urban park was scheduled for demolition, to be replaced by a simulacrum of historic military barracks and a shopping mall. A sit-in and encampment to protest the plans had been so severely repressed that soon protests had spread across the country, to be repressed in turn. The woman and her husband joined the *standing protests* now taking place: to stand, *with intention*, facing one particular direction. *You wouldn't know what you were looking at unless you already knew what you were looking at*, the woman writes.

x

A few days later, as many as fourteen million people are on the streets of Cairo, demanding the resignation of their new president, elected one year before.

A year before in the former Soviet bloc, protests were like this: a group of people gather in a park, shout *We are all just going for a walk,* then walk. In a park people begin clapping at a prearranged time. When clapping gets them arrested they set their cell phone alarms to go off all at once. Flash mobs perform folk dances or sword fights. A woman cooks breakfast in a frying pan over the eternal flame. At his trial one man protests that he cannot have been clapping: he has only one arm.

In Cairo the offices of the Muslim Brotherhood are set ablaze.

*

A friend writes from Cyprus: *I have just realized that the sounds I hear all weekend while bicycling near the DMZ are not cars backfiring.*

*

Her father's sister comes over for dinner bearing photo albums belonging to the aunt's aunt, her great-aunt. One album is bound grotesquely in Argentine cowhide. The great-aunt was in Buenos Aires during World War II, witnessed the revolution of 1943 from her window. This, *from her window*, is what the aunt says, and she thinks it an exaggeration until she sees the photographs: on the Plaza de Mayo a crowd of men in uniform, men in suits and slim ties, the camera quite close, their young and beautiful faces, open mouths. While there is urgency in the scene one would not know it as violent until a few photos later in the sequence, when a stand on the street is alight, foreground now a portrait of smoke. Upon flipping through the albums the word she thinks is *quaint*. Revolutionaries in suits. But what is quaint about the Infamous Decade? Or, another decade, another continent, 1,800 arrested for clapping? A flash mob arises only because no opposition may gather for more than an instant.

It is the age of the photograph: the nostalgia it cannot help but inspire, sepia tones and a quality of shadow, the revolutionaries' pronounced cheekbones and vivid eyes. How may one interrupt this impulse toward nostalgia, reject any pleasure before it arises, see a performance (in Russia, people tape blue buckets to their car roofs to mock government officials, with their flashing sirens and constant traffic violations) as not mere entertainment, not entertainment at all? How to see?

In her great-aunt's letters one may find such lines as this, from her travels in Paraguay: *There is a sullen pride on even the faces of the small boys and, though they may live like animals, one finds oneself wondering what they think about as they walk solidly along, and one has the definite impression that they do think. For example, look at the expression on the face of the woman in picture #11.* A photograph enclosed: women and children at market in white cotton dresses, two of whom face the lens, smiling, kneeling behind a spread of vegetables, in their faces a manifest joy.

She had wished to present the quotation as evidence of bigotry, a damning exhibit. But is it? With each sentence the sentiment widens, and the passage—though profoundly condescending—concludes in something like recognition of commonality beyond apparent difference, beyond the *prejudices of the time* (how many Nazis *did* her great-aunt know in Buenos Aires, the family often discusses). She cannot say what she herself would have seen, had she been in that market sixty years ago. How can she say what she would see now?

*

Her aunt hopes to collect the great-aunt's letters and diaries into a book; she has been told that surprisingly little remains from this era in Argentina, since Perón destroyed much of the archives. *An outsider's perspective would be very exciting*, a historian has said, or something to this effect. But is the story truly of interest, or just the sort of material each family accrues, each family discards or hopes to honor, tries to pass on?

Her aunt states that she herself is not enough of a writer to take on the task; she can't tell if this is meant as hint. If she is the writer descended from her childless great-aunt, her childless aunt, is this what she—just as childless—owes? What economy, a family—what code?

She might prefer not to remember that in at least one moral system the command to honor one's forebears ranks above *Thou shalt not kill.*

*

But why her own family, why not anyone's? What might she owe the women in that distant market, who smiled so radiantly at the camera, at the foreign woman behind the lens?

*

Her husband's sister turned thirty-eight this week. Her husband's mother is sixty. Certain calculations have grown more urgent since the death of the father six months before. The sister cannot feed herself, bathe herself, cannot use the toilet alone. She cannot be left alone, not even for the time it takes to go to the grocery store or the library. Lately she mistakes people she sees for people she knew twenty-five years ago, in another part of the country; she claims everyone she sees is wearing a wig or a mask.

How many years until the mother cannot care for the daughter? There are caretakers who may come for up to ten hours a week, the state has determined. The family is financially secure and lives in a nice house in a community that provides the sister some services; yet there is, she thinks, little mercy to the situation. The mother and sister cannot, for instance, simply move to be near the son: when one moves from one state to another, one often loses access to state services for the disabled and must join a waiting list that might be years long.

She and her husband would not take in the sister: this is one hard truth. Her care would require that one of them give up all other work; her care will become more complex as she ages. Lately she has been mistaking crumbs on the table or floor for her teeth. *My tooth fell out*, she says, and reaches.

Is this a washcloth or my brain? she calls out from the kitchen.

Is it cruel, to know they would not give their lives over as the mother has done? How deep the claims of blood? Not the right questions.

*

At every group home, how many residents go months without a visit? Couldn't anyone be of use?

*

And if your brother were building the bomb. If your son, your daughter, were the martyr.

A mother pitched a tent down the road from a president's ranch, hoping with her presence to end the war that had killed her son.

A man walked to the Pentagon with a wine jug of gasoline and his infant daughter. Did he set her on the grass at a distance, as some claim, or did the crowd seize her from him?

At the heart of three religions: Abraham leads his son up the mountain.

*

The sister, who loves conversation but cannot sustain it, often says, in reply to anything: *Really?* Instinctively one responds. Now she and her husband overcome any lapse in dialogue: *Really?*

*

In summer in the emergency room the CT scan shows inflammation in his abdomen, near the site of the anastoma. No, that's not where it was. The resident's nail polish was a creamy pink, not exactly a coral. The tender spot low to the left is caused by one or more inflamed lymph nodes. He is prescribed a course of antibiotics, the inflammation likely due to infection.

At his bedside she reads an anthology of short stories by veterans of the wars in Iraq and Afghanistan.

He has to wait hours for the CT scan, for the contrast he drinks to light up his gut. She goes outside to call his mother. She walks leisurely through downtown, in search of lunch. Everything costs more than she thinks it should, but perhaps she has not updated her sense of prices since she first lived on her own. This block serves the hospital; this block has three noodle places and a heap of clothes; here the lunch burger and fries are ten dollars and you can sit at a table on the sidewalk. Here the street signs bear rainbow flags and there is a *gay lawyer*, according to his sign, and a café she would have stopped in had the sole baguette in the basket not been collapsing in on itself. She chooses a wine bar that serves sandwiches; it's not what she would call her kind of place, if that could mean anything. Her panino bears perfect grill marks and to her surprise she orders an Americano. When her waitress is slow to bring water she feels she is suffering from thirst.

She and the waitresses are the same age. They are elegant in sundresses. She is aware that her limbs have been scored up in red welts by the branches that brush against her when she runs each morning on the trails through the city's beautiful park, which extends for miles along a creek and down to the river. If one wishes to have lovely arms, does one just not run in the woods? Her hair is still wet and in a large plastic clip. Could anyone eat such a large sandwich so laden with pesto without employing their napkin as she does? She props her book open under saucer and plate, scared to spill on it until she remembers it's hers.

The wedding colors were a fiasco, a young man at the bar says to his companion. Outside a man sends back one glass of white wine and another glass of white wine is carried out to him. The waitress and the man's date wear almost identical dresses.

Her husband has his own room in the hospital but there must be someone in a cot by the nurses' station outside the door.

Do you know why you're here? a woman's voice, the resident's, asks.

What city are we in? This the man answers in a mumble.

Do you remember being at the bar?

Why were you in the bathroom so long?

Do you remember being in the bathroom? What were you doing in the bathroom? The man will not answer. He confirms that he is taking his lithium. That morning he smoked a little pot.

The conversation repeats several times over the course of an hour.

Of the bathroom the man will say nothing. Her husband is discharged and they pass the cot as they leave the room. They had each been picturing a man with the look of a long-time addict, a man too long on the streets. But asleep on the cot is just a boy. He is curled up, one hand under his cheek, wears a nice pair of cargo shorts, a tee-shirt. Anyone would say he looks peaceful.

*

In Cairo revolution has resumed, or begun anew, or corrected its course. Or: there has been a coup. The president, leader of the Muslim Brotherhood, is out. To replace him the army has stepped in.

Various op-eds condescendingly remind the Egyptian people that they may not always like the outcome of elections.

The general now regularly on television, now self-appointed to lead the country, attended the US Army War College, which in rural Pennsylvania she had come to know by its gravel path, its adjectives, *friendly, courteous, responsible.*

*

If the millions in the street a decade ago shouting *no blood for oil* had been heeded.

*

If she were in Cairo, she imagines she would not cheer *The people and the army are one hand!* since this is not a sentiment she has ever felt.

*

But how, you may have wondered, could branches do such damage to one's arms, cause this fiery irritation? They can't. Not branches, but bedbugs. How slow they were to realize, though the sheets have been speckled with blood and for a week they have been idly killing insects with their fingernails or a pencil. They call an exterminator and in the nights before he comes they lay themselves in bed like pigs who take to the platter. She pauses between sentences and plucks a bug off her ankle to kill: the blood staining the tissue is her own.

*

In Cairo the army has opened fire on a crowd, or returned fire from a crowd. Fifty-one Islamist protestors are dead.

*

These boys, walking into schools or movie theaters or malls, gun in hand, how swiftly each disappears from the news. In the months since his capture, she has seen only one or two headlines about the younger brother. Despite what *Law & Order* claims, compared to the crime the law is no spectacle.

*

When not in church she cannot recall the liturgy; she remembers only two lines, from the intercession:

Call: *Lord let your loving-kindness be upon them*

Response: *Who put their trust in you*

*

On Facebook an Egyptian friend mourns the recent deaths of the protestors at the hands of the army; he writes *I have been able to place myself in the shoes of army officers shooting at Islamists and I must admit I would have fared no more merciful.*

SHE WENT TO church in high school and college, though her mother did not wish her to; or, her mother had doubts. When she was a girl they had attended as a family; she and her brother went to *Tuesday school*, where they learned Bible stories and sang along with the priest, who had bright blue eyes and played the guitar.

Light through stained-glass windows and the dull hours of sermons— memories whose general form she must share with who knows how many children. When young she misunderstood the emphasis of the Christ story and believed that God was dead. Had anyone asked her she would have said *God is dead*. She suspects she may have said this, which is how she was corrected. How common a belief this is among children she doesn't know; she should ask a priest.

She would kneel by her bed each night to pray. Children did this in books she read. Once her mother had discovered her in this posture and gathered her in her arms to explain—explain what? She did not understand and so cannot recall. She understood that her mother did not like prayer, or that she prayed; this thought shadowed their attendance at church, her decision in adolescence to return to church, though her family had not been in a decade. For a time her father came with her. There was not a hymn her father didn't know.

She can't remember what ended these expeditions, but she began to attend church instead with a friend from her high-school cross-country team. Each Sunday morning they'd meet at the early service, afterward go for their run.

When she was in college in a small town outside Boston she decided she would try the nearest Episcopal church, whose sign she had often run past. To her shock the priest there was the very same priest from her childhood, the blue-eyed priest of Tuesday school and the guitar. Nothing mystical, just that in the intervening decade he had moved. He looked much older, which should not have surprised her. She remembered him as joyful and often joking, which was not how he seemed now; but she remembered him from the hours he played and sang with the parish children.

She introduced herself to him one Sunday after service but he did not remember her. He must have known so many children. When she mentioned her parents' names he acted kindly as though he recognized them but she is not sure that he did.

A few years later the priest's son, who had been a friend of her brother's when they were boys, died of colon cancer. He had just turned twenty-five. Her brother had called the priest's son, or tried to, in the months before his death, though the two had not spoken since they were children. She has always admired this about her brother, since she does not know what anyone might have said.

In her memory, when she shook hands with the aging priest, who no longer knew her and had grown so solemn, his son was already dead. But when she checks the boy's obituary she sees this cannot have been true.

*

One expert describes cancer as a *microscopic rebellion*:

It is not so much a disease as a phenomenon, the result of a basic evolutionary compromise. As a body lives and grows, its cells are constantly dividing, copying their DNA... and bequeathing it to the daughter cells. They in turn pass it to their own progeny: copies of copies of copies. Along the way, errors inevitably occur....

Over the eons, cells have developed complex mechanisms that identify and correct many of the glitches. But the process is not perfect, nor can it ever be. Mutations are the engine of evolution. Without them we never would have evolved. The trade-off is that every so often a certain combination will give an individual cell too much power. It begins to evolve independently of the rest of the body. Like a new species thriving in an ecosystem, it grows into a cancerous tumor. For that there can be no easy fix.

*

According to his obituary, the priest's son had played the bass guitar—her own brother's instrument—in a funk-jazz band that was named for his father.

*

She hasn't yet mentioned that in the year between her husband's father's final two tumors—the one they operated on, the next that killed him—her own mother had had colorectal cancer.

*

As a girl she would daydream—can this verb describe the humiliating passions of imagination?—about being sick. Who might come to her hospital bed. How admirable her forbearance, her toughness. Not those words, but those sentiments. So frequent a fantasy was this that in later years she feared she may have brought on her own illness, or deserved it.

What she didn't know as a child was how absolutely illness may lack an audience. Few visit, few admire, because few see you at all. When you are well you are out with some friends, say, a few nights a week. When you are sick for months they do not call, or they call once. They may invite you to something, which you regretfully cannot attend, *I am sick*, and though you think they might visit they do not. A year later they say *Haven't seen you in a while!*

There are some signs that will yet command the audience's attention, their fear, admiration, repulsion. Cancer's bald head.

Conversely, anorexia is an unselfconscious performance. The anorectic rarely comprehends how thin she is; in her eyes she is fat.

(Upon her own recovery from anorexia friends had complimented her: *You look so good, you were so thin before!* She wanted to reply: *Why didn't you tell me?* But who would have understood?)

*

Lord let your loving-kindness be upon them

How self-contained the logic of this couplet. She likes to think that this intercession may be made by the faithless on behalf of the faithful, those who have tried to believe.

Who put their trust in you

*

Her counselor told her: when starving, the body begins to consume the brain. Among the first regions sacrificed is the one responsible for self-image, the ability to perceive the self.

*

You may not believe this, but when she transfers colleges—to another small liberal-arts college in another town in Massachusetts—she discovers that she knows the priest there too: he was priest at the Connecticut church she attended in high school. Wherever I move, she jokes, my priests follow. But she is slightly uneasy. Could this be a sign?

Or just a happy coincidence of the upper middle class? There are only so many college towns in New England, only so many Episcopal priests to staff them.

When in college she encounters her high-school priest—of whom she had been fond, on whom she and her friend had had something of a crush—she does not greet him, though she thinks he would remember her. She is at the pool when she sees him and like a child she ducks underwater.

Years later, she will finally attend his church. That Sunday he's not there; he is away visiting, they are told, the Holy Land. Some kind of peace delegation. The congregation prays for the victims on both sides of the wars in Iraq and Afghanistan, with an empathy that moves her. But she does not return, not in that town nor any other.

Her church-and-running friend, now a nurse, was already on Facebook when she joined, and sent her a warm note. From her friend's profile she reconstructs that in the last decade they had for a time lived in the same town; they had neither known of nor seen each other.

Every morning her mother would wrap herself in a shawl and walk out the back door, through the part of the yard fenced in for the dogs, closing each gate behind her. The yard backed up to the hospital parking lot and she could walk through the parked cars to her radiation and chemotherapy treatments. This was convenient if not simply necessary, since the daughter staying with her those weeks to help—the father had to travel often for work—was most days too ill to drive. The daughter stayed inside, watching the mother then the birds in the yard. Every time the mother left, the dog barked at the windows for a quarter hour.

*

This summer a whistleblower's trial draws to a close. A US soldier charged with aiding the enemy, he is responsible for the *largest set of restricted documents ever leaked to the public.* Before his trial he was kept for months in solitary confinement and on suicide watch, stripped of clothes and even his glasses, the restrictions upon him so severe that UN officials called them *cruel, inhuman, and degrading.*

In his statement before trial he described how he had initiated the leak: *[I] stated I had information that needed to be shared with the world. I wrote that the information would help document the true cost of the wars in Iraq and Afghanistan.*

He was betrayed to the FBI by an online friend—false friend, a better phrase.

Another whistleblower describes himself: *I'm no different from anybody else…. I'm just another guy who sits there, day to day, in the office, watches what's happening.*

*

When you think of those leaks, you too may think of that grainy video, cockpit footage of an Apache helicopter perpetrating a series of air-to-ground strikes in Iraq that will leave twelve civilians dead. Among the dead are two journalists: a photographer and his assistant, the photographer's camera mistaken for a weapon. After the first strike, in the second half of the film, a van pulls up to the scene and tries to rescue one of the journalists, who has been crawling away and is bleeding to death. The helicopters fire on the van, though its inhabitants are not armed and two of them are children.

The law might defend the initial strike: the US military would report that two RPGs and an assault weapon were found at the scene. Some argue, however, that one of the men bearing an RPG was the guard from the mosque down the street and not an insurgent. The strike on the wounded and unarmed journalist and the van of civilians presents a greater challenge. Just before the strike the American soldier pleas with his commander: *Come on, let us shoot.*

According to Wikipedia, a soldier later *seen in the video carrying the injured boy… became suicidal after the incident, and attempted suicide on two occasions.*

*

Well, it's their fault for bringing kids into a battle.

That's right.

*

Primum non nocere: a precept of medical ethics, and what could it mean beyond that? These words—*first do no harm*—do not appear in the Hippocratic oath, as she had expected.

Ahimsa: the principle of nonviolence. Tenet of Hinduism, Buddhism, Jainism.

The Jains, who famously sweep the path before them to protect invisible life from their footsteps.

Who cover their faces that their breath may not harm life forms in the air.

Strict vegetarians, all.

Jains pay their taxes.

*

After her military tribunal, at the start of her thirty-five-year sentence, the whistleblower reveals that she is a woman, not a man as she had been publicly known, as each reader of the news had known her, falsely. Does she in that moment know freedom? Has she slipped the yoke of history, which now bears the wrong name?

*

When she was twenty-one, twenty-two, she worked at an after-school program designed to *promote multiculturalism and nonviolence.* The administration and the majority of the staff were nonwhite, which has been true of none of her workplaces or graduate programs since: it seems her life has narrowed. These were the early years of her illness. When she tried to explain the situation to her boss, her boss said *you're lucky this is happening when you're young. You can still learn*—then spoke of her own health and how every day she drove to a pond in their town just to look out over the water.

It is the sincerity of the older woman's words that has proved memorable. She was young then and didn't know how rarely people would speak to her sincerely of suffering, how rarely she would do so herself.

*

Intention: everything and nothing. She had thought to minimize suffering and had failed: the cure to her illness manifested when she abandoned her vegetarianism, her veganism.

With a woman who was never quite a friend she had gone to a workshop at the local yoga studio; they were taught a practice called the *dance of Shiva*. Shiva, the Destroyer, the Transformer, she knows nothing. What relationship this practice had to anything Hindu she couldn't say. The movements were repetitive, meditative, not unappealing. She imagined a life this practice might be a part of, a life she knew she would not lead. Afterward they went out to a Belgian café for beer and fries. The almost-friend's boyfriend told a story in which it was not until he consulted a naturopath that he realized his chronic symptoms were caused by reaction to gluten—though he himself was a professor of nutrition science, and *how could I not have known?* Out of a general desperation, or to make conversation, she asked for the naturopath's name.

The naturopath—they only ever spoke on the phone—prescribed a series of tests and suggested that she try an elimination diet. She agreed. She'd tried such diets several times and so expected nothing.

This time, however, she surrendered her vegetarianism, as she never had before. For weeks she ate fish, sweet potatoes, greens, fruit, and felt entirely unlike herself: perfect. Her illness was triggered by—legumes? Absurd. Of all things. The humble bean: black bean, garbanzo, soybean, lentil, peanut. Once she stopped eating these she was suddenly, miraculously healthy. First for a week—it had been years since a week—then two weeks—how many years?—then a month—unheard of. Now it has been months, with some slight interruptions. It is another life.

Could she not have discovered this years earlier? Were there no clues? No doctor had mentioned this possibility. There was something newly undignified to this, to have been disabled by the innocent bean. The food children giggle at; staple the world over. She doesn't know what it might mean; she knows that she might have gone on for years without this revelation, since the series of events that led to it were circumstantial, themselves meaningless. She had been trying to make a friend; she had spent an afternoon doing yoga that bored her. Perhaps she had surrendered, but what, and to what? Her principles, to chance? How to think of those twelve years, suffering that could have ended at any time. The past.

How to think of herself, the sick one, *that girl*, she and her husband sometimes called her, a woman she had never wanted to be, had daily dreaded being. Whom she would love *never to see again*—this is the phrase she thinks, though she did not have to see herself: that burden lay with those who loved her or those whom she merely passed by. She saw the face in the mirror, colorless and exhausted; she saw the legs beneath her buckle, her handwriting slow to pained and childish loops. Yet it was she, the sick self she despised, who endured those immeasurable days, she who suffered each trial not knowing that relief would in time arrive. She.

How to speak of an *I* that is past?

*

Years she considered Buddhist law: there is reincarnation, but no self?

*

She once read an interview with another young woman writer, who upon being asked about her Buddhist practice said that she meditated but she had never *taken refuge*—the Buddhist commitment ceremony.

It was only upon reading these words that she realized she herself had made this commitment ten years before. She had been driven in a van to a monks' home outside Boston; she had received a scarf and a new name. She has forgotten the name; she had forgotten the entire night, the vows she took. The religion she dedicated herself to. Who joins a religion then forgets? She doesn't know.

*

The vigilance she now brings to her diet is new and old. The control, the attention—familiar. *Is there soy sauce in it?* she asks. *Peanut oil?* Now she eats what everyone eats: chicken and fish, turkey and beef. No longer the vegan's excruciating scrutiny: to open a menu and exclude all options but one. She has become normal; she has become unexpectedly American. For her birthday, the day before the nation's, they make burgers to grill.

Those years of anorexia she had dreaded the thought of being *normal*. A *normal weight*. When she knew women of average height and weight she didn't understand. Why not just lose a few pounds, so as not to be average? In her mind the beautiful was wholly opposed to the average.

She wonders if this madness had been an instinct misdirected, made monstrous. Food was making her sick even then; but she didn't know how, and her response assumed its own flawed logic, a logic that nearly killed her.

*

Of late the word *vigilance* echoes sinisterly, its kinship with *vigilante* exposed. This week the trial of the neighborhood watch volunteer ends and he is declared innocent. Over a year before, the man had taken it upon himself to follow a boy walking through the gated community in which both he and the boy's father's fiancée lived. The boy grew concerned at the vehicle following him; the man confronted him. An altercation ensued, its details disputed. Beyond a doubt it concluded when the man shot the boy in the chest.

The boy was black and had no weapon. In his hands, a bag of candy and an iced tea.

As the boy died the man mounted him and held down his arms.

According to the media, the man was white, or white Hispanic, or half-Peruvian.

According to the law, he acted in self-defense.

*

Meal by meal the vegetarian, the vegan, is aware of nonhuman suffering. She practices compassion. This compassion may become habitual, but it is still present in each choice, each trip to the store, each examination of a list of ingredients.

It is no longer practical for her to be a vegetarian. She selects the meat and fish she eats with care. And yet there's no question that—to eat their flesh—she thinks of animal suffering less. She feels farther from the animal world, as though before she was offering something she no longer offers. Her practice, her daily self. Yet now she is more like any animal, now that she will eat whatever she must.

*

A teacher once described the law of karma: if, say, a man were to kill a child. According to the law of karma, the child is being punished for misdeeds committed in a past life: he has earned this death. Yet, if there is *no self*, the child is not the one who committed these deeds. That self, that sinner, never more than a needed fiction, is dead and gone. So how do we understand the suffering of the child, the crime of the man? Buddhist ethics tells us we should feel compassion for the victim, since the justice, so-called, that he experiences has nothing to do with him. It is a law like the weather: the self is nothing in the teeth of the storm. We should feel compassion for the man, who will suffer in lifetimes to come for the evil he commits today.

Each of us a cloud formed and unformed by the wind of karma—this is hard to know as morality. She can't say if through the years she has grown nearer to understanding.

In the form of a man, the Buddha encounters a starving tigress with a new litter of cubs. He offers himself to her; he becomes her meat. He knows that if he does not she will feed upon her children.

In one version of the Jataka he reflects: *Suppose there were some criminal in abject misery and I took no notice of him even though I could be of help. It would be the same as committing a crime.*

And so he throws himself off a cliff to the rocks below.

We should not name this suicide.

*

Which *she* caused her illness, the one who meant to do good or the one who meant to harm herself? These selves do not of course exist: no one could distinguish between them, not even enough to name. There is only she, that exhausted pronoun.

*

If terrorism is a *disease of Westernization*. Blowback. Disease we cause, disease from which we suffer.

One suspects that to some the suffering is mere cost. To those men who would manipulate regimes; who would occupy a nation; who get their oil contracts and repatriate not a dime. To them it may be a matter of minimizing—containing—resistance, or the damage resistance inflicts. Blast walls. Surveillance. The Awakening Councils.

If terrorism is a disease, then in terms of pure statistics it affects few, at least in this country. May we accept a bombing here or there as the cost we cannot quite eliminate? An excess, one or two or twenty errant men, errant bullets, backpacks, planes?

*

Other odds may disturb more: if the current rates of incarceration continue, *one in three black men born today can expect to spend time in prison.*

*

Studies suggest that an immigrant is, for example, *up to five times more likely to be diagnosed with schizophrenia than a white British person*. As explanation some theories had blamed the trauma from which immigrants had fled, or the trauma of migration itself. But rates of mental illness, schizophrenia especially, are even higher worldwide in the second generation, those children of immigrants born in the new country. Or, new to their parents: to them it's home.

*

An article reports that the older brother's wife, who was born in America, began after her marriage and conversion to Islam to cover herself and to speak with an accent.

*

A later investigation will assert that the brothers' motivation for the bombing was not political but personal. Not that of global jihad, but *rooted in the turbulent collapse of their family and their escalating personal and collective failures.* One doctor suspects the older brother of schizophrenia; for years he had told his mother he heard an angry voice within him, *inside his head, someone who wanted to control him, to make him do something.* It felt like *two people inside of me.*

If, the article muses, the bombing was born of *private motives*, that would make the brothers *homegrown murderers*, like the other young men—young white men—whose deeds we know well, whose deeds we unwillingly recognize.

*

Her own father is the eldest of five, three brothers and one sister. The youngest brother was born healthy, but when as an infant he contracted meningitis his brain was damaged. He has been disabled since. Neither she nor her mother has ever met him; her father almost never speaks of him.

Her grandfather was a surgeon who ran his practice from the family home in New Jersey. When evidence began to emerge about the dangers of smoking, he quit. But his wife never did, and she smoked through five pregnancies. When her youngest boy fell ill, she feared that her habit had weakened his immune system and so she was in part to blame. At least this is the grandmother's story as she, the granddaughter, has always known it; when one day she repeats this to her father he does not confirm it. The rest of the children, he notes, were fine. The grandmother herself cannot be questioned; she died a quarter century ago of emphysema.

When she imagines her father's childhood, there is a quality of chaos to the scene, a tumble of children and cats, tennis rackets everywhere, patients waiting in the hall on the leather easy chairs her grandfather favored, the smell of smoke deep in the wallpaper. As a boy her father rode a bus over an hour each way to private school; the four children attended three different schools. The youngest was cared for at home, then placed at age six in an institution.

Why couldn't she quit smoking? she asked her father of his mother, when as an adult it occurred to her to ask. He can't say, but suggests as explanation the grandmother's feeling of inadequacy when compared to her sister, the world traveler and investigative journalist whose archives the family continues to explore. The grandmother had gone not to college but to secretarial school, and as a wife in the New Jersey town of *a Hundred Millionaires*—as it was then known—may have felt burdened by the need to represent her family, its name, the wealth and status it had established by laying oil pipeline across the Midwest and West.

Why don't we visit him? she asked later of her mother, meaning her uncle. Whose absence she had accepted as a child, but had later come to question, when she'd learned that her cousins visited him regularly, as did her uncles, her aunt. Her mother couldn't say.

Her mother and her aunt both have offered, as explanation, that the eldest and youngest brothers looked the most alike. *It's upsetting for your father*, they told her, *to see his double…* To see his double what?

In time she visits the uncle herself. It's a sort of pasta-lunch open house at his center, and she meets her aunt, her uncle, her uncle and his new girlfriend there. They've brought gifts, which the youngest brother likes to unwrap. They've brought balls, which he likes to play with.

He looks like her father; he looks nothing like her father. All five siblings (and she) have the same lanky frames, angular faces, aquiline noses, light blue eyes. The same square-palmed, large-knuckled hands, which they wield in surprisingly like gestures. The youngest brother's face is drawn in on itself and into an underbite. He looks like one of them, but disabled. His walk shares the energy if not the authority of his brothers'. He prowls the dining area, hard to keep up with, though he must be fifty-five. When a boy, her father says, he used to run at walls and bash his head into them over and over. He does not speak; he has never spoken. The sounds he makes are to some degree intelligible to the staff. She sits at the table with his brothers and his sister and she believes he knows her as one of his own. He takes her hand and leads her to a door. He wants to go outside, her uncle says. He always wants to go outside.

She supposes this must serve as reconciliation, this Diet Coke taste in her mouth, this slow walk with middle-aged siblings around the institution's grounds, her uncle turning wordlessly to wait whenever someone falls behind.

Later in conversation her father will trace his way back into family history she had not known: Your grandfather, he says, was a doctor and captain in the army, stationed in the Philippines while the US prepared to invade Japan. He did not see combat. Mostly he patched up his fellow servicemen after bar fights, that sort of thing. For all we know, he said, our family owes its existence to the nuclear bombs dropped on Japan.

Think about that, he said.

So she did.

*

Photographs from the battlefield at Gettysburg were, notoriously, falsified. This she learns long after visiting the memorial and its exhibits. Falsified not by a curator's hand, but the photographers themselves. The dead in one photograph named Confederate, in the next Union: nearly a century later it would be proved these were the same dead; only the position of the camera has changed. Another photograph famously captures a sniper dead in the *sharpshooter's den*. But his weapon is not a sniper's, and this same man may be seen fallen elsewhere on the slopes. It seems that the photographers lifted this corpse into a more picturesque location, arranged his limbs, his gun.

These facts alter our sympathies not for the corpses so much as for the photographers, who have framed falsehood in the guise of truth.

War feels to me an oblique place, Emily Dickinson wrote to Colonel Thomas Wentworth Higginson in 1862.

*

In the same letter the line before reads: *I should have liked to see you before you became improbable*. Transplanted this seems better elegy than most for the boy who now sits in a prison west of Boston, a few restrictions recently lifted, his trial yet to begin; after long delay it's announced that he will face the death penalty.

*

What are we to do with the gift of survival?

Daily into the wound we thrust a pinchful of gauze.

A son sets off in search of his father. A drone finds the father, a drone finds the son.

On the fields by the graves of the Carlisle Indian Industrial School children play soccer or lacrosse. The graves face away from them but bear their names.

Legend claims that the first man to run a marathon died at its end. He ran from the battle where the Persians had been defeated to the heart of Athens. *We won!* he cried out and fell dead.

One winter she spent a week confined in a hospital in Boston that overlooked where the finish line would be come spring. For a week they read her brain scans, then released her; having discovered nothing unusual, no clue to her illness, they declared it must all be in her mind.

A true story.

April–August 2013

II

*"The public realm, as the common world, gathers us together
and yet prevents our falling over each other, so to speak"*

*"I, being where his blood's no longer flowing,
or where the shipping lanes cross"*

IN THE NAME of civilization, foreign governments refuse to sell us the chemical needed for lethal injection.

I told the boy this, the pronoun his to judge.

It was after the first World War, I added dutifully, that an excess of gas production resulted in the widespread use of the gas chamber.

The boy's curls were shorn and he was fattening. He had promised me an exclusive interview, but so far I felt as excluded as ever. His letter had been to the point. On the envelope bearing my reply I had given my return address as 18 West 11th Street; in what at least seemed ignorance the boy did not comment.

Of course I'd sent him my novel.

Each time the lights flickered his jumpsuit grew brighter.

I blinked. In a slow loop in the windowless room a fly droned. The fly was, we could safely conclude, a drone.

Those are the ones, I said aloud, that can land on any microwave, any power line, and recharge.

The fly landed on the camellia pinned to my breast. The flower was dead.

Shall we begin? I said. I began:

We have two pressure cookers packed with ball bearings. Then the guns, and several cars. Two nylon backpacks. We might call the backpacks a *double-edged blade*, since they allow authorities to identify us.

Ball bearings have been in use since ancient times, I said—information I'd had to research—although not primarily as weapons.

I was surprised, I added, at their size.

There was an elbow pipe wrapped in black tape, I said. To project the photo I clicked a clicker. Blood clouded a street's rough surface, blood red and darkly clotted.

Fusing elements made from toy cars.

In 1921, I said, the artist announced her intention to stop painting. The bourgeois distinction between art and industry must be erased. In 1924 the artist died. Nothing to do with the Revolution or its aftermath. She caught scarlet fever from her infant son. The relevant principles for our discussion are *tektonica, konstruktsiya,* and *faktura.* How appropriate the use of these materials with regard to their given purpose? How may we erase a bourgeois distinction?

For example, I said, if you were sent to Guantanamo, you wouldn't even have to change clothes.

I was wearing what you might call a romper, a coincidence the boy noted with only a nod.

A nod and a smirk?

The boy rubbed his injured hand. When he finally spoke, he narrated the course of the genocide known in the Caucasus as Operation Lentil, his tone something less than disinterested. Tens of thousands of Chechen and Ingush had fought in the Red Army against the Nazis. Yet after the war, the Soviets condemned the whole population as collaborators. There was an insurgency; soon half a million were deported; however many died in the roundups, the deportations, in exile. Chechen gravestones were plucked from the earth to be used in Soviet footpaths and pig pens. Town after town lost its name.

Is this—I interrupted—*faktura*? Is this story material?

The boy glanced at my notes, which I failed to conceal. In blood I had written *I can't stand to see such evil go unpunished.*

*

Not everything is about you, I said. Even though I was with him again, for hours had practiced his smirk in the mirror. Everything has to happen to someone, I noted. I realized I was trying to explain exactly that principle which his actions testified he did not comprehend.

Listen, I said:

On the way there I smoked a dozen cigarettes, I know, because I stopped one short of thirteen. Each had nothing to do with the next; my desire for each was new, even perfect. My satisfaction was nothing; I don't know if I ever felt satisfaction. In the back seat again and again the boy smacked his palm against the window. We were passing a field of cows, all lying down, and though the sky was clear the cows were right, later it would pour down rain.

The drive was one hundred miles. The boy was six years old.

Six is so very young, I said aloud.

What? my husband said. I tried to think if he was usually more polite; if at other times he said *beg your pardon?* or *I'm sorry?* I could not for the life of me recall.

I knew the boy's two blankets and suitcase were in the trunk, but my hands looked to smooth them. Instead I inspected my stockings for runs. How was there not one run?

Now the boy banged Pups's head against the window. Pups's nose always tucks to the right when under duress. A quirk of the stuffing, surely, but the consistency of the gesture provides character.

Yesterday my husband had been called in to surgery, right at lunchtime. I had just opened a can of soup to warm on the stove. He put on his brown corduroy jacket and canceled the afternoon's appointments. I didn't know what to do with the soup; I had already had a small Waldorf salad and the boy had finished his bologna sandwich. He was so thin that lately I added extra mayonnaise, which I did not know if he liked—a small frustration, but I felt it. I poured the soup, cream of mushroom, into a dish, two slimy mushrooms falling on the stovetop I had just wiped clean, falling with malice.

We had put the suitcase and blankets and Pups in the hall to await our departure. The boy kept lifting Pups off the pile; Pups lived on his bed. Back and forth all day we moved the soft brown dog.

My husband returned late and always I attend to how he closes the door, changes into slippers, walks to the refrigerator, pours a beer into a glass, and sits in the leather easy chair everyone else finds stiff; the rhythm of his movements discloses whether the surgery has gone poorly, usually because the motorcyclist was not wearing a helmet. He is called in for the motorcyclists because he is good with burns, and although it's dreadful to think of, that's what the road does. Burns down the skin as one skids. That night I tried to think how his ritual differed with a good outcome, but I could perceive the difference only if I did not think of it. I was up reading, later than I meant to be. But how could I sleep?

In the morning, though he too had barely slept, he said he would drive. We reached the home in good time. I would not look at the other residents; I would not waste attention on any boy but my own. My own—we would not be permitted to see him for one full month, so that he might adjust to his new life. We closed the trunk. The boy would not be embraced; he was screaming and he wriggled free. When they advised us to leave, we left. Through the rain the pastures stank. Rain darkened the highway and the smoke tasted good.

*

Sometimes the boy and I sit a long time—what feels like an epoch— without speaking. I want to tell him that my silence is not born of fear. I want him to know a silence of which he may say nothing because it is mine. This is not a desire that those who observe us can recognize. Their gazes are distracted by the fly in the corner: again and again it rams itself against the wall. This is neither personal nor political. There is no silence; there is the noise of the fly. What did it sound like when after the ransack of Baghdad Tamerlane's soldiers assembled pyramids of skulls? It's true that silence is something the boy and I have in common, or not. I offer it to him and, eye for eye, he responds. If he speaks I do not flinch. I suppose I offer him only my face, which I could not witness for the long hours he has, and from which he does not avert his eyes.

*

Not everything is about me, the boy said. He meant something like this:

The boy slid off his backpack. He stooped to remove his math text-book, which he tried to store on the locker's top shelf, but couldn't. What the fuck? There was an empty bottle of blue Gatorade, though he only drank yellow. There was an empty half-size Pringles can and a pack of rolling papers. No, there were no more rolling papers. You shouldn't share your locker combo, he thought, with assholes.

He tore a piece of paper from a notebook, wrote on it *This is not a rolling paper*, put it in the empty bag and put the bag in Kev's locker.

I'm giving up smoking, he'd told the girl last night. No, he'd tweeted it at her. In his memory he'd told her, her head against the dark paneling by their booth, her finger moving red pepper flakes over the table's surface, but that had been another night, a night he hadn't spoken to her. I'm giving up all that shit, he said.

Dawg, try not to talk to yourself at like ten in the morning, Mike said behind him. No, on second thought, maybe that's cool. Like, anyone can talk to themselves at ten at night, but ten in the morning is hardcore.

You know it, the boy said, and pushed his hair from his eyes, a gesture he'd been trying to lose.

The girl had come by his locker yesterday and said, Smells like gym socks! even though it didn't, he never even kept his gym bag here. Then she'd said, How do you do your hair without a mirror?

On reflection, these were both shit comments. One was just a cliché and the other was cutting him down, but in a clichéd way. So why was he into her?

She wasn't boring. She tilted her face toward the TV. He watched her watch the news in the corner, her eyes greener. He thought there were tears in her eyes. It wasn't that they were all stoned, that wasn't it. People think being stoned is something it's not. That's not what it's about.

When he tries to remember her now her eyes have gone blue like the eyes of the woman across from him, the so-called writer.

That's not right. Memory is fucked, he thinks, because now if he tries to picture the girl he's just making her up.

After everything happened she gave a long interview, crying, but was it bullshit?

He was late for practice and slipped through the halls. He liked moving fast like this, not even time to say hi, stopped just once to flip Kev's hat off his head by the brim. *Opportunity, diversity, respect* read the wall the hat hit. The girl was hooking up with a guy on the basketball team, he'd heard, but it wasn't serious. It probably wasn't even happening. The girl had a perfect laugh. Every now and then, she'd say something. It could blow you away, the shit she said.

Fuck America.

The girl's hair was golden but he'd lost her face. He couldn't remember her face. He didn't know what she'd said. It had been another time, when they were on smoke break at driver's ed. She'd said something, something like, how she felt most vulnerable when she was driving. Like, the car's body was so loose around you, and your body was soft, just flesh, just sitting there, singing. Anything could happen. It's the most dangerous thing you can do, she said, getting in a car. He thinks that's what she said—she touched the sleeve of his jacket. Maybe she remembers everything.

*

Like any nation, I had priorities. I was training hard; I would be a drone pilot. Not rogue so much as freelance. I knew I'd tell the boy when I first dreamed in infrared. The anticipation kept me awake. My days passed in dark rooms and my nights seemed not to pass.

It was like this: I was in a dark room. It was not a dream. Watch. On the screen before me a field, figures in the field. Confirm. I had received all necessary intelligence. For hours static caressed voices at my ear. I was authorized to strike. I was the author of the strike. The field exploded. White and gray. In the field it was the day before the holiday to celebrate the sacrifice Ibrahim would have made, knife stilled at his son's throat. It's a bad day to be a fucking Taliban, I said. Though it was much like any other. The target of the strike was one grandmother, who had been picking okra with her grandchildren. That's all I'm asking. Scattered over the field was one grandmother. Into a mouthpiece I limned the scene. The okra wouldn't pick itself. In every dream I would watch the woman bleed out.

*

In the novel, the boy said, his head propped up on one hand, you don't describe how they make the bombs. What, did you just not want to Google it?

No, I said. I mean: yes, I didn't. But anyway this was years before we knew about the government's internet surveillance and I wouldn't have imagined it was as bad as it is. Or I'd have liked to be on some watchlist somewhere, a hard target for a white girl to hit. Anyway I didn't care to convince anyone that I'd done my research. Anyone who wants to build a bomb can.

Sure, the boy said.

You of all people should agree, I said, unnecessarily.

Make a Bomb in the Kitchen of Your Mom, I said. Sounds like bad English, but the authors spoke good English.

Pressure-cooker bombs are rare here, I said, compared to in Pakistan and Afghanistan. First, because all bombs are rare here, and second, because pressure cookers are so much less widely used.

I myself have one, I confessed, and I've never understood it.

I asked the boy: How American was the bombing? How do we measure its Americanness? By drop of blood?

There have been no shortage of bombings to which it may be compared.

For the sake of his posture I shoved his elbow off the table. I said: I didn't describe the bombs because I didn't want every terrorist who read the book to nitpick. *Everyone's a critic,* I said—air quotes implied.

I said: Autopsies suggest that you killed your brother. He had been shot but he died when you ran him over. He'd run out of ammunition; his body was dragged through the streets when you tried to ram the cops and flee the scene. If he had been able to speak—could he still speak?—he might have said that this was what he wanted. Not to be taken alive.

He might have said something else.

Police report that they were trying to drag him to safety when you drove away, pulling him—or his body—with you.

The boy's eyes were damp. All these feelings are normal.

Now, I said, the ones who lost their limbs, they're still alive.

The boy knew this too.

In the blink of an eye the fly was on the table between us. As it bided our time I asked: What would it matter if your brother had been, as the internet claims, trained by CIA-funded programs, if the workshop he'd attended during his last trip abroad was paid for from our coffers? Would this make his actions less American or more?

Cui bono, I asked, if Muslim dissidents overthrew Russia's control of the North Caucasus and aligned the region with the US-allied Wahhabi governments of Saudi Arabia and Qatar? Who would build the pipelines?

We have so much to talk about, I said. But on this we differed.

Sometime later he said: It's chickenshit that you didn't write about building the bombs. It means you didn't have to imagine the bombs.

If I'd imagined them, I said, if I had pictured just what they'd do, would that make me more or less like you?

That's what I'm saying, he said.

*

On the train out of the city I pass the paved yard of a jail. An inner and outer fence enclose it, inner curved inward at an angle that from above would resemble the jaws of a beast in a '70s sci-fi flick. In the gullet, a basketball court. Some men play, the rest watch. When I pass they do not arrange themselves in postures beautiful though abject: the gray and blue of their jumpsuits, dark skin, radiant asphalt, silver fence, fading background of brick, ball mid-air, a hand poised in follow-through, foot aloft. The train passes, my face only one at its hundreds of windows, all speed and sentiment. Crowning each fence are loops of barbed wire. What tests were performed to ensure that no man could scale a fence thus curved, toss a leg then himself over the barbs, find himself triumphant if bloodied on the far side? How many have made it over the first but not the second? Peter Fechter was only eighteen when he was shot while crossing to West Berlin. Over the course of an hour in no man's land he bled to death. Both sides watched.

Your opponent is awarded points if you commit these infractions.

I asked: Do you consider your silence to be a form of *engaged withdrawal*?

I feared the boy might claim a victory; I might retreat to the moral high ground only to find him there, occupier, chuckling as he tossed up blast walls. When I had been trying to demonstrate the idea that *revolutionary action is "not a form of grim self-sacrifice"* but rather *"the defiant insistence on acting as if one is already free."*

When wrestlers meet they shake hands, bodies curved to guard the ground between their feet.

For two full seconds the scapulas must touch the mat.

Boys in track suits bounce in place. On command in pairs they grapple. Music plays.

In the video the circle is smaller than I thought, the boys smaller. Night after night I watch the boy. He twitches his spandex uniform back down his slick thigh. I cheer for or against him.

The boy and I found ourselves in a common situation. Alphabet on the table, fingertips on the planchette. By whose hand would the revelation begin? We wished to hear from the same spirits but our questions parted ways.

The hands may touch but not overlap.

The planchette is shaped like a teardrop.

They say the truth lies in the *ideomotor response*.

I have found the truth lying elsewhere.

*

Tell me what words you first learned in English.

Now forget them.

When and of what did you first dream in English?

In your dreams who would you say is a foreigner?

Write those names down.

Across the wall the fly tracked an efflorescence of blood, I could not for the life of me say whose.

*

The fact that the US has administered the death and homicide of over one million civilians in Iraq—

This sermon, I said to the boy, is dated October 2001. It's as though the cleric expects us to remember the war before this one.

—does not just justify the killing of one US civilian in New York or Washington, DC.

And the deaths of 6,000 US civilians in New York and Washington, DC, do not justify the death of one civilian in Afghanistan.

Only 3,000 died that day, fewer than 3,000. It is in our casual relationship to facts that the cleric and I may be most similar, and yet it is for this quality that I most condemn him.

That sentence isn't true.

The difference between a bomber and a drone is a face.

What justified the death of one US civilian in Yemen, in this case the cleric himself?

No need to answer.

When you think of that spring, when you remember, when you try to remember, what happens next?

You've said that you chose the target only a day or two before-hand. Let's not read too much into it.

If you can feel this, please try to remember.

One night, I confessed, my brother walked all the way through the Callahan Tunnel.

Should I say: one night, in a state of desperation, my brother walked all the way through the Callahan Tunnel.

Every driver in Boston lay on the horn.

Let's say you committed to something you cannot recall. The river was no muddier than usual. You cannot say now if it was faith. You fingered a scarf at your neck; you concealed your hair. If you could you would take refuge in memory. Let's say there is the fact of the past. You know I do not mean only the day of the murders. Every day we have lost.

*

The boy has threatened a hunger strike, but I'll beat him at his own game.

Between us the table was blank, sun setting. The fly alighted on the curve of his shackles, the fly circled, starved for a phone.

The great thing about being force-fed, I said, is that they rinse the tubes out for you.

He offered: Did you know that *factoid* has two contradictory definitions?

Do you know who you're talking to? I said.

Do you know who I am?

The boy hollowed out. His breath stank and the plane from hip to hip grew concave. His face grayed, his face would break first.

Don't mistake the marathon for a sprint, I told him.

Not a strike, I said, but a siege.

I'd surpass him; I'd take sandpaper to the canvas.

I bore magazine after magazine of warm carbs.

I swear to you I was winning.

In my arm a flaw had occurred. In the flesh a deep impression, a perfect circle. Circumference silver; mere blood. The boy looked to the drone: wrong again. Wait, I whispered. In the dark finally a white cloud burned.

Clear the flesh from the path of the light.

According to the news, I said, the activists were *shot like dogs*. What were the dogs shot like?

The boy's gag reflex was a live wire. Me, I carry a stick of gum.

Don't say I wasn't a good sport.
    Don't trust anyone, I told him. Not Willie Pete. Not the brain, not the bowels.
    Think about everything you can get away with.
    I did.

The boat's wake: blood.

It's called mirror punishment, I explained to the guards. It was on the way to their supervisor's office that my foot broke. We all heard the snap. Out of respect they said nothing.

When the air cleared, the plate sat between us, untouched.

Even this croissant, I said, testifies to the discord between our peoples.

By placing confidence in violent means, one has chosen the very type of struggle with which the oppressors nearly always have superiority.

Did you think, I said, that you'd last on the boat? That one Saturday they'd grab a can of nightcrawlers and a six-pack and there you'd be? The tarp your heavens, bullet clenched between your teeth?

The shock waves feel, it's said, like a wall moving through air, a wall intact when it meets the body. Bodies.

Weakly he said: You keep mixing your metaphors.

I said: *The term "political defiance" originated in response to the confusion and distortion created by equating nonviolent struggle with pacifism and moral or religious "nonviolence."*

In other words, I said, the difference between a privateer and a pirate is the gibbet.

I no longer bleed. When the fly comes for me, the bluest air.

My mouth waters.

After exhaustive evaluation they concluded: the boy and I were neck and neck. We were at the end of our rope. When the guards closed their eyes, they could not tell the difference. I pinched at the boy's humerus. In my cheeks the crescent mark of his thumbnail. When we abandoned the difference between limbs we felt a burden lift. At each other's throats we felt a pleasure.

My feet kicked air.

When the guards came for us, the boy bit. It was then that I knew I would win.

In pools on the asphalt clouds formed his face. Through his face fleetly a shadow.

To his face I said not a word.

Not one.

III

March 2015–

BUT TO COME back, *hoc opus, hic labor est*. Pain in the shoulder, pain in the gut. A fever is a month of fever. If cancer enters the bloodstream in the colon, it arrives at the liver. Where is the pain in the gut? Where is the liver? The tumor lends a firmness to the abdomen, there. A year ago, a spot on a scan, not followed up on. It couldn't matter. Could it matter?

The tumor is thirteen centimeters in diameter.

Before the doctor she and her husband sit. Later they may know what it means when the doctor says: *I have seen people come back from things like this.*

Mornings you awake alone and find him asleep on the floor. This is the only place he can sleep. To reach your desk in the dark step over his form on the floor.

NOTES

9: Emily Dickinson, letter to Thomas Wentworth Higginson; Norman Mailer, *Armies of the Night*, quoted in Amy Clampitt, "The Dahlia Gardens."

12: Elias Khoury, *Gate of the Sun*, trans. Humphrey Davies (New York: Archipelago Books, 2006).

24: Rebecca Solnit, "The Longest War," TomDispatch.com, January 24, 2013.

30: Jeremy Lazarus, president of the American Medical Association, writing to Secretary of Defense Chuck Hagel, April 25, 2013.

37: Susie Orbach, *Hunger Strike: The Anorectic's Struggle as Metaphor for Our Age* (New York: W.W. Norton, 1986).

39–40: "Hunger Strikes at Guantanamo Nearly Double," *Al-Jazeera*, March 19, 2013; Paul Harris, Tracy McVeigh, and Mark Townsend, "How Guantánamo's Horror Forced Inmates to Hunger Strike," *Guardian*, May 4, 2013.

46: Lyn Hejinian, "Two Stein Talks," in *The Language of Inquiry* (Berkeley: University of California Press, 2000).

53–55: Project for a New American Century, "Rebuilding America's Defenses: Strategy, Forces, and Resources for a New Century" (September 2000); David Ray Griffin, *The New Pearl Harbor: Disturb-*

ing Questions about the Bush Administration and 9/11 (Northampton: Olive Branch Press, 2004).

57–58: Ward Churchill, "Some People Push Back: On the Justice of Roosting Chickens," September 2001.

74–75: Christian Caryl, "The Bombers' World," *New York Review of Books*, June 6, 2013.

79: Marcy Wheeler, "Dzhokhar Tsarnaev's Search Motion: The Reddish-Brown Powder and the Pizza Papers," May 9, 2014, and other posts on her blog *emptywheel*.

80: Conor Friedersdorf, "How Team Obama Justifies the Killing of a 16-Year-Old American," *Atlantic*, October 24, 2012.

80: Rainer Maria Rilke, "The First Elegy," *Duino Elegies*, trans. Stephen Mitchell.

81: David Stuckler and Sanjay Basu, "Why Austerity Kills," *New York Times*, May 12, 2013.

82–84: Tana French, *Broken Harbor* (New York: Viking, 2012); Denise Mina, *The End of the Wasp Season* (New York: Reagan Arthur, 2013); Henning Mankell, *Faceless Killers*, trans. Steven T. Murray (New York: Vintage, 1997).

85–87: David A. Fahrenthold, "Boston Marathon Bystander Says He Acted Instinctively," *Washington Post*, April 16, 2013; Tasneem Raja, "These Soldiers Did the Boston Marathon Wearing 40-Pound

Packs," *Mother Jones*, April 16, 2013; "Peace Activist Carlos Arredondo Hailed as Hero for Aid to Boston Marathon Bombing Victims," *Democracy Now*, April 16, 2013; Trymaine Lee, "A Father with a Coffin, Telling of War's Grim Toll," *New York Times*, February 1, 2007; Elise Forbes Tripp, *Surviving Iraq: Soldiers' Stories* (Northampton: Olive Branch Press, 2007), chap. 29.

92: James Dao, "Researchers Find Biological Evidence of Gulf War Illnesses," *New York Times*, June 16, 2013.

96–98: "Putin Meets Angry Beslan Mothers," BBC News, September 2, 2005; Yaroslav Lukov, "Beslan Siege Still a Mystery," BBC News, September 2, 2005; Anatoly Medetsky and Yana Voitova, "A Reversal over Beslan Only Fuels Speculation," *Moscow Times*, July 21, 2005; Nick Paton Walsh, "One Year on, Beslan Mourns Its Dead and Demands the Truth," *Guardian*, August 30, 2005; "Beslan Militant Gets Life Sentence," *Guardian*, May 26, 2006; David Satter, "The Truth about Beslan," *Weekly Standard*, November 13, 2006; Mike Eckel, "Video Reopens Debate over Beslan Attack," *USA Today*, July 31, 2007; C.J. Chivers, "The School," *Esquire*, March 14, 2007; Ivan Nechepurenko, "Decade after Beslan, Questions Remain Unanswered," *Moscow Times*, August 31, 2014.

108–111: "Jeremy Scahill on Paris Attacks, the al-Qaeda Link, and Secret US War in Yemen," *Democracy Now*, January 12, 2015;

Jeremy Scahill, "Inside America's Dirty Wars," *Nation*, April 24, 2013; Daniel Klaidman, "Exclusive: The Awlaki/Tsarnaev Connection," *Daily Beast*, April 26, 2013; David Johnston and Scott Shane, "U.S. Knew of Suspect's Tie to Radical Cleric," *New York Times*, November 9, 2009; Mark Mazzetti, Charles Savage, and Scott Shane, "How a U.S. Citizen Came to Be in America's Cross Hairs," *New York Times*, March 9, 2013; Craig Whitlock, "U.S. Airstrike that Killed American Teen in Yemen Raises Legal, Ethical Questions," *Washington Post*, October 22, 2011; Conor Friedersdorf, "The Killed-at-16 Transparency Test," *Atlantic*, May 28, 2013.

117–118: Amy Clampitt, "The Dahlia Gardens," *The Kingfisher* (1983); epigraph by Norman Mailer.

119: Adrienne Rich, from "Shooting Script," *The Will to Change* (1971).

120: Ellen Barry, "Sound of Post-Soviet Protests: Claps and Beeps," *New York Times*, July 14, 2011.

126: Roy Scranton and Matt Gallagher, eds., *Fire and Forget: Short Stories from the Long War* (New York: Da Capo, 2013).

135–136: George Johnson, "Why Everyone Seems to Have Cancer," *New York Times*, January 6, 2014.

142–143: Chris McGreal, "Wikileaks Reveals Video Showing US Air Crew Shooting Down Iraqi Civilians," *Guardian*, April 5, 2010;

"Permission to Engage," documentary film in *Witness* series, *Al-Jazeera*, July 10, 2014; Raffi Khatchadourian, "No Secrets," *New Yorker*, June 7, 2010.

153: Nick Harvey, "The Shocking Link between Racism and Schizophrenia," *New Internationalist*, October 10, 2011.

154: Sally Jacobs, David Filipov, and Patricia Wen, "The Fall of the House of Tsarnaev," *Boston Globe*, December 15, 2013.

158: Jim Hicks, "Observers: The Real War and the Books," *Lessons from Sarajevo: A War Stories Primer* (Amherst: University of Massachusetts Press, 2013).

163: Hannah Arendt, quoted in Maggie Nelson, *The Art of Cruelty: A Reckoning* (New York: W.W. Norton, 2012); Rob Halpern, *Music for Porn* (Callicoon, NY: Nightboat, 2012).

165: James Merrill, "18 West 11th Street," *Braving the Elements* (1982).

191: Robert Creeley, "Heroes," *For Love* (1962).

This book draws upon many minds and sources; a few others deserve particular acknowledgment:

Patrick Blanchfield, for his thinking on gun violence, on his blog *Carte Blanchfield* and elsewhere, and for directing me further toward Derrida and on drones; Jacques Derrida, "Autoimmunity: Real and Symbolic Suicides," interview by Giovanna Borradori, trans. Pascale-Anne Brault and Michael Naas, in *Philosophy in a Time of Terror: Dialogues with Jürgen Habermas and Jacques Derrida* (Chicago: University of Chicago Press, 2003); Robert Emmet Meagher, *Herakles Gone Mad: Rethinking Heroism in an Age of Endless War* (Northampton: Olive Branch Press, 2006); Maggie Nelson, *The Art of Cruelty*, which this book quotes or converses with multiple times; Janet Reitman, "Jahar's World," *Rolling Stone*, July 17, 2013; Gene Sharp's pamphlet *From Dictatorship to Democracy* (available through the Albert Einstein Institution, www.aeinstein.org) and the article that led me to Sharp (Sheryl Gay Stolberg, "Shy US Intellectual Created Playbook Used in a Revolution," *New York Times*, February 16, 2011); Peter Sloterdijk, *Terror from the Air*, trans. Amy Patton and Steve Corcoran (Cambridge, MA: Semiotext(e), 2009).

ACKNOWLEDGMENTS

Gratitude ever to Zach Savich. Thanks and tribute to Sydney Landon Plum, Terry Plum, and Kathy Savich.

I wrote this hoping Caryl Pagel might like to read it, and she's done one better, as she does. Thank you to Caryl and the team at Rescue Press, with whom it's an honor to work: Daniel Khalastchi, Sevy Perez, Alyssa Perry, Zachary Isom, Kelli Ebensberger.

For insight into earlier drafts, thanks to Pam Thompson, Jenn Mar, and Fady Joudah.

I'm grateful to the *Seneca Review* for publishing an excerpt, an early encouragement. Thanks to Roy Scranton, at whose invitation it was a pleasure to share this project at AWP 2014. Thanks, too, to Edie Meidav and Chelsea Hogue for including an excerpt in the forthcoming anthology *Strange Attractors*.

Thanks to friends old and new—those in Philadelphia who welcomed us, those from near and far who appeared.

HILARY PLUM is the author of the novel
They Dragged Them Through the Streets (FC2, 2013).
With Zach Savich she edits Rescue Press's Open Prose Series.
She lives in Philadelphia.

RESCUE PRESS